Teaching Spanish

Teaching Spanish

A CRITICAL BIBLIOGRAPHIC SURVEY

Herschel J. Frey
University of Pittsburgh

NEWBURY HOUSE PUBLISHERS, Inc. / ROWLEY, MASSACHUSETTS

NEWBURY HOUSE PUBLISHERS, Inc.

Language Science
Language Teaching
Language Learning

68 Middle Road, Rowley, Massachusetts 01969

ISBN: 0-88377-021-0   (cloth edition)
        0-88377-029-6   (paper edition)

Printed in the U.S.A.   First printing: March, 1974

Foreword

This is the first published bibliography of Spanish applied linguistics and teaching methodology. As a teacher of Spanish, I have long felt that teachers of Spanish at all levels, as well as foreign-language education researchers and textbook writers, would appreciate a critical survey of the literature in those areas in which the application of linguistic insights would be both practical and enlightening. Foreign-language teachers have become increasingly aware of the importance of keeping up with advances that relate directly to the improvement of teaching skills and materials. Understandably, this has not been, nor will it likely ever be, an easy undertaking. Along with constant dialogs with colleagues, keeping abreast requires a great deal of reading. But it is simply impractical and time consuming to go through library card catalogs or work through current and back issues of the growing number of professional journals. The purpose of this annotated bibliography is therefore to provide teachers and researchers with comprehensive descriptions of primary studies in a convenient format, thereby reducing the amount of time required to review the literature of Spanish applied linguistics.

A glance at the Table of Contents reveals that a wide range of categories has been included. If somewhat arbitrarily selected, the categories nevertheless reflect the interests and vital concerns of the profession as expressed in the literature, and these considerations guided me in selecting appropriate categories. Though some of the entries might conceivably be included in more than one category, most have one principal focus. In compiling this bibliography, I have had to review hundreds of articles and full-length studies, the majority of which are taken from recent literature. The more than one hundred critiques represent only about one-fourth of the total sources considered. Thus, rather than include most or all of what has been written concerning Spanish applied linguistics and the teaching of Spanish, I have instead been selective. Studies of either peripheral interest or questionable merit have been excluded. This approach avoids needless duplication or the inclusion of materials that have been superseded. Personal testimonials, especially those concerned with familiar classroom techniques, and reports of studies that are either inadequate in experimental design or too limited in scope have been omitted.

Quality of scholarship and usefulness were the principal criteria applied in the selection of entries. Unpublished papers, dissertations and other source materials not readily available are not reviewed. Critiques of dictionaries, word counts, dialect studies (other than general treatments), and background or highly specialized studies are also not included. Unfortunately, several items I would like to have consulted were not available. Nonetheless, the studies that are included seem to me to constitute a representative list of the best that has been written in this dynamic and fast-developing field.

A list of bibliographies and selected works on the structure of Spanish appears in the Appendix.

Full descriptions of each entry were preferred to shorter and perhaps more superficial commentaries in the belief that this would provide more useful information. Many of the articles and books are cross-referenced. In addition, book reviews are cited for some of the longer studies.

The critiques are not intended to replace the original sources. But anyone who reads this volume carefully will, I think, acquire an awareness of the many areas in which linguistics has a direct application for the improvement of second-language teaching—here, specifically Spanish—and of the current state of research into the relationship between linguistics and language teaching.

In preparing the critiques, I have endeavored to maintain a steady objectivity and not impose my own linguistic and pedagogical persuasions in such a way as to misrepresent the authors' intentions. However, a critical survey necessarily requires comment and judgement, and my personal views show through, doubtless even in places and in ways of which I am unaware. The responsibility for these views, as well as for the selection of all entries, is entirely my own. I should like to apologize in advance to any whose original thoughts I may have misrepresented and express my gratitude to all for their unique contributions.

It is my hope that the description contained in this survey will serve as a guide to teachers and researchers both in locating up-to-date information for the improvement of classroom instruction and in identifying productive areas for research.

I should like to express my indebtedness to the late William E. Bull of UCLA for his encouragement and always good advice, and to my wife, Harriet, who typed the manuscript and offered many valuable suggestions.

Since this is the first critical bibliography to be published in Spanish applied linguistics and methodology, there are doubtless ways in which it can be improved. It is in the hope that such improvements can be incorporated in future editions that I invite any and all critical suggestions and reactions.

H.J.F.

June, 1973

CONTENTS

INDEX TO JOURNALS

ESJ	*Elementary School Journal*
FLA	*Foreign Language Annals*
Gl	*Glossa*
Hisp	*Hispania*
IRAL	*International Review of Applied Linguistics*
Lang	*Language*
LL	*Language Learning*
MLJ	*The Modern Language Journal*
PMLA	*Publications of the Modern Language Association of America*
TESOLQ	*TESOL Quarterly: A Journal for Teachers of English to Speakers of Other Languages*

I. General Studies

1. BARRUTIA, RICHARD
    "Linguistics and the Teacher of Spanish and Portuguese," in *A Handbook for Teachers of Spanish and Portuguese*, edited by Donald D. Walsh. Lexington, Mass.: D.C. Heath and Co., 1969, 20-35.

A general, easy-to-read survey of recent developments in linguistics and their application to the teaching of Spanish and Portuguese. Barrutia acknowledges the importance of separating what we know from what we do not and realistically assesses the major contributions of linguistic science (theory) to FL teaching (practice).

In singling out principal discoveries especially of descriptive and transformational or generative grammar, the author cites linguists and their works, and examples of how this information has been put to use in textbooks. He discusses phonemes, morphemes and syntax and provides examples from Spanish. Two similar and related methodologies which evolved from the thinking of teachers and applied linguists are outlined: audiolingualism and the fundamental skills approach. Barrutia demonstrates how these methodologies are variously realized by teachers. The role of the NDEA Language Institutes is also considered.

Discussed also: the advances and refinements in articulatory phonetics; word classifications and their functions; pattern drilling.

Though the person who has read in linguistics and language teaching will find little that is new here, others will appreciate this excellent summary. Appended is a useful (if careless) and partly annotated bibliography.

2. BARRUTIA, RICHARD
    "Some Misconceptions about the Fundamental Skills Method," *Hisp*, 49 (September, 1966), 440-446.

Strong answer to an article by T. Earle Hamilton, "The Audio-Lingual Method in the University: Fad or Panacea?", in this same issue of *Hispania*, pp. 434-440, in which Barrutia vituperates his adversary for "pernicious pontifications" on audiolingual teaching. In attempting to set the record straight, Barrutia accuses Hamilton of everything from naiveté to the worst kind of deliberate misinterpretation of the facts.

Perhaps Hamilton's gravest sin, according to the author, is a thorough misunderstanding of the term "audiolingual," and especially his insistence that in theory and in practice it excludes a place for the written skills. Barrutia produces sufficient evidence to disclaim this notion and emphatically avers that no competent applied linguist has ever endorsed so one-sided an approach. Hamilton is guilty of other misrepresentations: that audiolingual students are to learn the FL as they did their mother tongue; that they need no understanding of grammar; that the "natural" and new-key methodologies are in great part based on the same principles. Barrutia patently rejects Hamilton's conclusions based on the statistics gathered from diagnostic and other standardized tests administered to students at the Texas Technological College. He questions the testing procedure of this "ill-conceived experiment" and cites counter findings.

In defending the fundamental skills method (FSM), Barrutia quotes from other articles, whose authors are similarly guilty of misunderstanding audiolingual, new-key, linguistic, etc. teaching. (Barrutia uses these terms interchangeably.) What he finds most objectionable is the fact that these detractors are the least knowledgeable about the method they are criticizing, and that they seem determined to attribute to this teaching method features which are not nor have ever been a part of it. Barrutia lists and refutes seventeen specific objections to audiolingual teaching brought out in one of these articles.

Concludes with the hope that practitioners of the new methodology will not be as close-minded and intransigent as are the traditionalists.

3. BARTLEY, DIANA and ROBERT L. POLITZER
   Practice-Centered Teacher Training: Spanish. Philadelphia: The Center for Curriculum Development, Inc., 1970. xiii + 186 pp.

This manual for the training of Spanish teachers was developed in the Stanford University Secondary Teacher Training Program. It is intended for use in both the retraining and the original training of FL teachers. The stated aims of the syllabus are "(1) to bring about a much closer integration of the language practice, applied linguistics, and methods element of the teacher-training courses, and (2) relate them directly to the practice element by introducing the device of *micro-teaching*." This orientation is based on the concept that a well-integrated program should provide the trainee with adequate information to relate each lesson in applied linguistics to a corresponding lesson in language practice, principles of methodology, and specific micro-lessons to be taught by the participants in the training program.

Part I. A compromise, in outline form, between a review grammar and a rundown of the structure of Spanish, including phonology. Only the main facts are brought out, with native-language interference described for involved sounds, structures and vocabulary. Not intended to replace any of the existing manuals on applied linguistics, Part I is instead a guide for the person responsible for teacher training. Very few of the descriptions could be considered complete but they do constitute a basic inventory for further investigation. The approach to grammar is quite traditional and does not reflect some of the important advances made in this field. The teacher trainer will find useful the topical index to some eight studies in Spanish (applied) linguistics.

This section on Spanish linguistics is marred by some misleading or faulty information. For example, the phoneme /d/ is given as a principal ending for masculine nouns. Some of the rules are incomplete in that they fail to account for usage of high functional yield, including what is often described as "exceptions" to the norm. On the other hand, the authors accomplish in sixty pages about as much as can be reasonably expected.

Part II. A description of suggested teaching behaviors which characterize the performance of the master FL teacher. This information is meant to serve three related purposes: research, evaluation, and training. According to this outline, a teacher's performance should be evaluated as to: 1) audiolingual activity, 2) presentation of basic material, 3) teaching of structure, 4) teaching of pronunciation, 5) teaching of sound-letter correspondence, 6) teaching of reading, 7) teaching of culture, 8) using visual aids, 9) use of electronic equipment, and 10) making homework assignments.

Bartley and Politzer give in this section brief discussions of each of these activities. While audiolingual procedures and the role of the teacher are clearly stated, more attention could have been paid to underlying theory, a prerequisite to know-how in modeling, drilling, correcting, etc. Appropriate emphasis is placed on the necessity of liberated expression as real communication, but preceded by also necessary basic and controlled practice.

Part III. Micro-lessons and how to teach them. This is the trainee's culminating experience, prior to taking over a real class, in which all his other study and training find a practical application. Indeed, the teacher can be expected to successfully micro-teach only after he has mastered the material in Part I (linguistics) and Part II (methodology).

The thirty-one sample micro-lessons described and outlined in this section are *real* lessons, and include the teaching of a wide range of language components and activities—sounds, grammar, dialogs, songs, etc.

There are obvious advantages to using micro-lessons. They force the practice teacher to concentrate on one teaching problem. The micro-lesson is short and usually represents no more than one-fourth, or less, of a given day's activities. Specific performance criteria are established; thus the teacher can be evaluated and can judge for himself, especially when the model lessons are video-taped. These lessons, though carefully structured, admit modification, such as the teacher must allow in the actual classroom. The authors suggest that the student participants be slightly ahead of the level of the material, to insure a smooth operation. This kind of teacher preparation has become quite popular and the only significant limitations seem to be the degree of effectiveness of the supervisor (or model teacher) and the availability of props, including the video-tape machine.

There is much to recommend this practical manual. Even the experienced teacher will learn from it, and there are abundant aids for the teacher trainer and the beginner.

[Reviewed by Anthony Papalia in *MLJ*, 56 (March, 1972), 191-192; and by Wallace J. Cameron in *Hisp*, 55 (May, 1972), 396-397.]

4. BROWN, MARGARET J.
   "A FLES Research and Experimental Project," *Hisp*, 48 (December, 1965), 890-894.

This is more than a report of the results of an experimental project initiated in the University Elementary School, University of California at Los Angeles, to identify the optimum age for beginning the study of FL. It is a thoughtful résumé of the personal philosophy of a sensitive and highly successful teacher of Spanish.

One hundred and sixty-four elementary students and one high-school class of first-year Spanish participated in this study during one year. The experiment yielded two principal conclusions: 1) upper elementary-school students can learn a FL readily, and therefore the time spent in acquiring a second language can be justified, and 2) students at this level learn well with the same goals, materials, and method used at the secondary level.

Brown's finding is that the special characteristics of a successful program suited for learners of widely varying ages support what is currently known of learning theory. In fact, the principles of learning as translated into practice were obvious to those who observed the demonstration classes.

The teaching approach was eclectic. Contrastive analysis was used in devising the materials and in teaching, but Spanish was presented from its own point of view. Liberal use was made of William E. Bull's *A Visual Grammar of Spanish*, and in general his particular application of linguistics to the teaching of Spanish was followed. The material and the activities of each class session were controlled to the point of becoming programed. The homework assignments were programed, written to be self-instructional, self-pacing preparation, rather than reinforcement of partially learned material. Memorization was kept to a minimum so that the time saved could be more profitably used in expanding control of communication.

Other characteristics of these experimental classes: Students were taught to "listen fast" to Spanish spoken at a normal rate and respond spontaneously. While emphasis was on the target language, English was not banned from the classroom. Economy determined the choice. All information was concise, precise, and linguistically accurate—and given before any drill. Performance in all four skills was the program objective. There was no pre-reading period. Good pronunciation habits were insisted upon. The multimodal approach, less demanding on the teacher than, say, a constant stream of oral drills, was intended to reach more students.

Interested visitors, as well as the students, were pleasantly surprised at the attained level of linguistic sophistication. These youngsters were not only producing correctly and consistently the allophones of Spanish /d/, but they were also able to discuss the phenomenon.

The experimental materials, originally developed for beginning secondary students (grades seven through twelve), proved to be easily handled by younger students, suggesting little if any correlation between achievement and age. Achievement tests revealed evenly proportioned distributions for each age level.

Brown sums up her excellent report by suggesting that a separate type of program is not needed for FLES, if pacing and size of learning increments are properly controlled.

5. BULL, WILLIAM E.
   Spanish for Teachers: Applied Linguistics. New York: The Ronald Press Co., 1965. vii + 306 pp.

This and the combination of Nos. 35 and 70 are the only "full" studies of Spanish applied linguistics. However, the authors differ considerably both in approach and in the kind and quantity of material they cover. While on the one hand Bull offers more information and opinions regarding the nature of language learning in general, Stockwell, Bowen (and Martin) provide greater detail, if not always depth, in studying Spanish phonology and grammar (meaning syntax)—especially the latter. The treatment of morphology is much the same, but, unlike Bull, the other writers take a generative approach in analyzing grammar. Other differences: more examples from English and a hierarchical view of student problems in Stockwell *et al*; Bull is more interested in "how the Spanish speaker organizes reality;" and his writing style is more deliberate, methodical. Both studies have in common a pronounced concern for contrastive analysis as a useful means of pointing up differences between the native and target languages.

Chapters 1 and 2 are Bull's introduction. These some forty pages constitute a fine summary of the nature and current status of the art of FL teaching. The problem with these introductory chapters—and all that follow them—is that they contain a wealth of information ("truths") in synthesis form, and the student who is new to the topic must read two and three times to get at all the information, other than simply memorizing it. Bull perhaps anticipates the student's problem in discerning the central points and issues and wisely includes for each chapter a lengthy list of very useful questions. Unfortunately, many of the questions are not sufficiently clear, and the frustrated student will come to class with questions about the questions. And elsewhere, in the body of the study, Bull loses the student from time to time in a style made profuse by complexities of logic, as the author gets involved in lengthy and complex analysis. These moments are not all that many, however, and the student is better off for having thought through each argument or presentation, and this keeps the teacher on his toes as he must be carefully prepared.

For the most part the author's introductory remarks are sound and are established in a simple and direct style, characteristic of this applied linguist. But only time will tell if, for example, this statement is to hold up: ". . . when the time factor is kept constant for all four skills, the method is not the factor that ultimately determines success" (4). Chapter 2, "Basic Facts and Fundamental Principles," represents a comprehensive discussion of the many central issues involved in the area of FL teaching, including language and dialect, the principle of contrast, segments, symbols and words, the extra-linguistic elements in communication, interference in second-language acquisition, hearing, speaking, reading and writing, etc. Here and throughout the book Bull does everything that he can to separate orthography from speech, for years of teaching have convinced him of the necessity and the difficulty of understanding and maintaining the distinction when analyzing the language.

Chapters 3 through 6 present the sound system of Spanish. The only thing missing is a more complete description of the sounds of English. Especially the advanced student will need a more thorough knowledge of the native-language phonology. Bull first establishes the necessary distinguishing sound features and in general rightly stresses the importance for the teacher of a firm command of articulatory phonetics as regards Spanish and English. Before getting involved in the subtle differences between sounds and how each is or isn't operationally contrastive, the author gives a clear presentation of phonemes and allophones. Once the student has understood this basic information (Chapter 3), he can more easily go on to the next chapters and, step by step, come to understand all the principal phonological features of Spanish, including those of intonation. Some teachers will question the validity of the environmental conditioning of some of the allophonic variants posited by Bull for his (generalized or normalized) dialect of Spanish, but he stresses only the commonly acknowledged ones. And in general he is careful to spell out the specific dialect area for each allophone. The student will appreciate the summary steps given for each sound: identity, distribution, interference, and spelling.

The chapter (5) on the semivowels and semiconsonants is as complete as the teacher will need. In fact, some will be confused and get lost in the subtle, though mostly cogent arguments put forth to establish the contoid or vocoid identity of the familiar "semi-" sounds in Spanish.

"Intonation is the stepchild of the language classroom" Bull declares (Chapter 6) and he then proceeds to give this ignored but important area of phonology its due along with the segmental sounds of the language. The reader will recognize here the familiar, accepted intonational patterns for Spanish.

Chapters 7 through 23 treat almost exclusively Spanish grammar, beginning with morphology. Particularly good is the discussion of words, morphemes, inflection and derivation. Less complete is the chapter (16) on syntax, but in truth much of what Bull has to say in the last part of his book deals either directly or indirectly with syntax. Throughout the sections devoted to the grammar of Spanish the author uses with considerable success certain unique linguistic terms of his own invention. Some of these serve a purpose principally for analysis, though others are obviously used for their pedagogical application. Once the student has successfully gone through Chapter 8 and mastered the system of agreement and "matching" used by Spanish, he should have no real problems in understanding the rest of the text.

One source of difficulty, however, is the Spanish verb. We are given the morphology in Chapter 8, though it is not until after several intervening chapters on quite different topics that we have a final analysis of the system (Chapter 14). Students find this chapter the most difficult of all. This is due in part to the student's own lack of insight and is, to an extent, Bull's fault. (For example, he could have omitted the confusing diagram on p. 156, and elsewhere in the chapter certain points could be made in other, more clearly stated ways.) All in all, however, students who understand Bull's analysis of the Spanish verb system feel they have accomplished no mean feat, and, indeed, it represents an understanding of many moving parts which the student often has not looked at at all or in quite different ways or only for English. Any way you slice it, literally, the Spanish verb is a mess, and few linguists who have thoroughly studied the forms end up agreeing, even with their own analysis. For, unless one is willing to posit a liberal number of zero morphemes, few suffix phonemes are left to carry multiple signal loads. But Bull has "solved" the problem as best he can—and perhaps as well as anyone can, and his "slots" and categories serve the needs of the materials producer and the teacher who must understand, use and adapt these materials.

A good and thorough description is given for the indicative and subjunctive in Spanish, and the student will profit from reading the chapter (12) on linguistic "sets" and "systems." The author confuses the reader on at least two occasions in this chapter, when he fails to maintain clear distinctions between his categories. Other than the chapter on the verb system, the ones which are likely to present the greatest problem of understanding are 17 ("Mathematical Organization of Entities") and 22 ("Prepositions and Adverbs")—the latter, because prepositions and adverbs are always troublesome and because, in some cases, Bull tries to create patterns of usage which are difficult to see. The author saves the best for last: *ser* vs. *estar*. In a very short chapter Bull manages both to dispel some old and prevalent erroneous notions about these two most common of all verbs and to demonstrate their occurrence, including the overt and covert cues for choice.

It is a shame that the author chose to omit from his study a chapter establishing the forms and uses of drills. While Bull defines the pattern drill and on several occasions suggests a specific drill for a given teaching problem, nowhere in this otherwise excellent study does he treat the topic at any length.

A useful index is provided for reference.

[Reviewed by J. T. McCullough in *Hisp*, 49 (March, 1966), 177-178.]

6. BULL, WILLIAM E.
    "We Need a Communications Grammar," *Gl*, 2:2 (1968), 213-228.

An article which recognizes the increasing need for competent people who can teach languages to a shrinking world, but whose educational system has not been and is not now structured to meet this need.

The author cites the various massive experiments utilizing the "New Key" FL teaching methodology as proof of the fact that professional leaders have found no way to diminish the number of frustrated teachers and students. Though he does allow that now at least all students who survive their language courses learn to speak the FL (a questionable admission), Bull, echoing comparative results given by others, maintains that it appears unlikely that any greater number of our students are learning to speak the FL than did students in the traditional, direct-method course (again, a specious tabulation based on unavailable data).

Only the role of linguistics, as a primary factor in this disheartening development, is discussed in this article. In weighing the two possible explanations for our programs not having produced the desired results, Bull quickly concludes that limitations of the contributions formal linguistics was expected to bring to FL teaching, rather than any inadequacy of pedagogical philosophy, explain the failure. But he is not too eager to fault the descriptive linguist, who brought neither experience as a FL teacher nor much (or new) knowledge of learning theory to the problem. Inevitably these linguists turned to their methods and findings based mainly on the descriptions of exotic languages; such could not, Bull correctly points out, provide the answers to the vital questions regarding format and procedure for new teaching programs.

In pointing out the folly of expecting grammar rules which follow the pattern drills they explain to somehow teach that which the student was unable to absorb via these drills and memorized dialogs, Bull cites the less common practice of giving no rules at all, in hopes that the student will somehow discover on his own how the language system works. Either of these two *modi operandi*, the author argues, produces what he labels a "deficit of knowledge," which frustrates the learner and understandably often causes him to give up entirely.

Not only are we expecting too much, according to Bull, but we are deservedly getting too little. Since the linguist has yet even to discover (much less formalize) the language rules which account for, say, near-native fluency, our students have no recourse but to call upon their "intuition," perhaps somewhat in the same ways they acquired their first language. And even if the linguist could supply the descriptions, it would be the system that would be described, not the process of message sending–which is Bull's main concern. The author can conceive of no adequate teaching grammar (i.e., "communications grammar") that does not go beyond this limitation and that would not reveal to the student how two people communicate. Such a grammar would provide, among other things, an understanding of the following:

1) The specific social (personal) relationship between speaker and hearer, including the experiences of both;

2) The status of shared knowledge (i.e., the shared focus within the universe of discourse);

3) The nature of reality and its organization;

4) The geometric relationship of entities in space; and

5) Culturally determined usage.

In delineating these areas, Bull provides convincing examples from Spanish. He discusses the matter of six vs. two (for English) sentence pattern possibilities when three syntax blocks (*Los dos muchachos estaban jugando en el patio.*) are involved, and for which no existing grammar has posited the necessary systematic rules which might lead the learner to discover the appropriate or preferred pattern, given the context. Bull uses this good example sentence to demonstrate the at first not apparent but numerous examples of linguistic and non-linguistic information, both semantic and syntactic, which the learner must control if he is to make correct choices based on available cues. It is one thing to discover that the Spanish lexicon contains no real equivalents for the nouns *pet* and *yard* (around a house), but information concerning the ways speakers of Spanish organize the world—which can explain such differences between native and target languages—must be made available to the student if he is to control the FL with any degree of accuracy.

Bull does not claim that he possesses any blueprint for this new communications grammar (or even a working sketch of a possible model), but his outline of the five points that merit detailed exploration would suggest the strong possibility of productive results.

7. CÁRDENAS, DANIEL
     Applied Linguistics: Spanish. A Guide for Teachers. Second Preliminary Edition. With an introduction by Simon Belasco. Boston: D.C. Heath and Co., 1961. v + LVII + 62 pp.

In his Preface the author readily admits to the less-than-completely careful planning of this and the companion volumes (for French, German, Italian, and Russian—all under the general editorship of Simon Belasco), and he explains that the exigencies of a deadline to meet the 1961 opening of the first NDEA Summer Language Institutes precluded the kind of final version he would have preferred. But, given the inestimable value these applied linguistic introductions held for the participants in these institutes, one would be wrong to criticize this or the other volumes out of their intended context. Most if not all linguists and methodologists who participated in these teacher-training institutes can look back and recall the paucity, indeed all but total lack of usable material for their courses. Further, it is not unlikely that these Heath studies provided many an instructor with an introduction to the general topic of applied linguistics for the particular language he taught.

As one of the first studies of its kind, appearing some years before near-full linguistic analyses were available for English and especially Spanish, it is only natural that this manual is incomplete in detail and approaches outline in its format. If not comprehensive, the manual is at least practical. Problematic for the authors was the constant reminder that their audience, the institute participants, included both teachers and students at the same time, representing very heterogeneous groups.

Contents: Introduction; Syntax; Morphology; Phonology. The Introduction by Belasco succeeds rather well in establishing the rationale behind pattern practice. But rather than an introduction to linguistics or teaching methods, it is a guide for teachers. It is primarily concerned with introducing those structures likely to appear in basic dialogs and the pattern drills that rework them.

Belasco gives a good early definition of the applied linguist and does his best to outline the boundaries that separate linguistics from pedagogy. We can only conclude that many teachers have ignored or misunderstood what Belasco meant ten years ago, when he stated that "the responsibility of the structural linguist ends when he uncovers the patterns. But whose responsibility is it to take the patterns and present them so they can be taught effectively. . .? It would be ideal if the language teacher could do it. Someday he will!" (II-III) The Introduction also contains sensible discussions of grammatical hierarchy, syntax, and word classes. An especially useful feature is a series of questions accompanying each discussion—the answers to which directly follow from, but are not mere rewordings of, the introductory explanations. Appended to the Introduction is a Selected Bibliography that contains items of mainly general information on the nature of language.

The second part of this manual, by Daniel Cárdenas, presents the principal structural categories of Spanish and suggestions on how to present them to students. The emphasis is based on the findings of contrastive analysis, which provided the writers information regarding predictable interference the American student is likely to experience in learning Spanish. The treatment is nowhere near as exhaustive as several studies now in existence [See Nos. 5, 35, and 70], but as an outline the information adds up to a rather complete general inventory. That which is new (by 1961 standards) is a systematic presentation of syntactical, morphological, and phonological—in that order—problems based on native vs. target language analyses. Phonology is not presented first, in the belief that the instructor would tend to prolong its study and thus create boredom and frustration.

The sections on phonology and morphology are more complete than the treatment of syntax. The syntactic information is presented mainly as structural-descriptive (Pike's slot-class correlation technique), rather than transformational rules.

Most of the more familiar teaching techniques are included. Cárdenas used as his criteria in deciding just what to include the results of a poll he conducted among a group of teacher trainees asked to list the points which had been the most problematical to them in their teaching experiences. Not surprisingly, the number and nature of the problems did not vary significantly. Rules rather than exceptions to the rules are established. Along with the explanations, problems for discussion and specific references are given.

The weakest features of this study include inadequate descriptions of the pattern drills and their primary (and secondary) functions, questionable analyses of Spanish noun morphology, and the presentation of the basic Spanish sentence types. Better and understandably more complete is the last section on phonology. Even a quick once-through of the "Selected Spanish Bibliography" evinces the numerous and important addenda available to the student and the teacher ten years after this pioneering, worthy effort.

8. FELDMAN, DAVID M. and WALTER D. KLINE
    Spanish: Contemporary Methodology. Waltham, Massachusetts: Blaisdell Publishing Co., 1969. vii + 191 pp.

As one of the relatively few studies treating exclusively the methodology of teaching Spanish, this handbook differs from the others in its comprehensive coverage, in some depth, of the central questions of language-teaching methodology. In stressing general considerations of methodology, rather than applied linguistics, it offers no full and inevitably necessary inventory of specific problems in teaching Spanish to speakers of English. Although the role of contrastive analysis in FL teaching is well outlined and a strong case is made for its usefulness to the teacher, except for phonology (Chapter 4), the structures of Spanish and English are not developed, and the teacher will have to look elsewhere for this information.

The authors present, in rather familiar outline, a brief history of language teaching in this country and an explanation of how each of the various methods has in its own way broken ground in adding new insights into the language-learning process, leading to the current fundamental skills method. In keeping with the generally acknowledged usage of this term, Feldman and Kline imply orderly and inductive learning of the four skills in the established sequence, but with more and perhaps earlier emphasis on the written skills, and including oral fluency as liberated expression, true communication.

One should question the accuracy of the statement that transformational grammar has "promised to add new dimensions to the currently practiced methodology" (vi). While it may well be the case that some teachers and methodologists have anxiously awaited new and revealing applications of generative grammar to teaching procedures, in general linguists have been careful to caution language teachers not to expect ready answers to central problems from the insights of generative grammar. Throughout their book the authors seem on the verge of overstating the linguist's ability to help the teacher. The authors should have instead explained how language's most demanding characteristic (its creative aspect) presents the teacher with apparently contradictory methodological considerations: how to "control" the student's growing linguistic competence, while at the same time encourage him to develop the creative range of the language. Another topic not included is ways to expand the classroom situation and provide a larger, more valid language-learning context. Incomplete is the thumbnail description of "indispensable qualifications" of a competent teacher—model, judge, and drillmaster (7).

In summarizing the achievements of the traditional grammar-translation method, with its (exclusive) emphasis on the written skills, the authors have exaggerated the probable results: a student learns a second language "first as something to read, then as something to write" (11). In these traditional classes the typical student did not, by any meaningful definition of language use, *learn* to use the language, any more than do the majority of our audiolingual students learn, after two years of language instruction, to use it orally.

At the present time it appears difficult to expect our students to attain the authors' major objective: "to understand and speak the language as it is used in its culture" (14). However worthy this goal may be, given the usual limitations of class size, contact hours, etc., we simply are not prepared to accomplish so much.

A good point, and one worth stressing (32), is that in the early learning stages no student should be asked to imitate another as his model. Also sound is the advice that the final student version of the language segment should be followed up with the teacher's echo version. And the authors rightly emphasize setting a fast pace, even if frustrating in the early weeks. Another student frustration, and one that many teachers are willing to justify in the long run, occurs when written materials are outlawed, thereby removing a much used crutch for our typically eye-minded students. Interesting also is the question concerning the best ways to teach dialog meaning. The authors do point out the obvious drawbacks of supplying the English version of the dialog, but there is no discussion of the not uncommon practice of providing the colloquial English equivalent, along with some of the more literal "meanings" set off in different type. Questionable is the economy of introducing the new dialog via a short prose summary, which can turn into the type of guessing game the beginning student cannot afford to play.

Only Chapter 4 ("Phonology") offers a rather complete teaching outline, and even it is incomplete in discussing and establishing appropriate drills for the vowels.

Described in Chapter 5 are the relative merits of the pattern drill types, including the increasingly less popular combined pattern replacement drill, criticized for its puzzle-like make-up. It should be pointed out, however, that this drill, complicated though it can be, could well prove to be quite functional. Admittedly, this drill does (especially for Spanish) stress superficial concordance, but the student must *first* recognize and classify information about the cued item and perhaps generalize about the grammar and the context of the item in terms of the drill sentence. A strong case is made for the correlation drill and its function in fixing the patterns of language agreement. And the item substitution drill is defended as productive in establishing the semantic range of an item, along with its grammatical combinatory potentials. Unfortunately, this chapter on drills offers only a weak presentation of the transformation drill. Lacking also are suggestions for teaching the more subtle grammatical distinctions.

In Chapter 6 ("The Language Laboratory") we are told that a new methodology has been developed toward finding ways to more constructively use the lab, but we are never told what it is (Teach? Reinforce? Introduce? Expand? All of these? How?). Also unanswered (Chapter 8) are many questions regarding effective testing, especially of the oral skills. The truth of the matter is that many of our current tests focus strongly on the more easily handled linguistic situations (synonyms, antonyms, paraphrase, vocabulary associations, etc.), and the test items are reduced to mere exercises in logic, rather than true language competence. Drilling or testing, we seem to be faced with the same problem; namely, too much stimulus, too little free response of the student's own making.

The teacher is provided some good suggestions for first- through fourth-year audiolingual sequences (20-26). Some teachers doubtless will not understand several of the suggested techniques, and certain parts of the outlines are too skeletal, but the activities for each level are practical, varied, and well articulated.

To the person familiar with the notions of contemporary methodology, there is little in this handbook that will be new or revealing. On the other hand, with the exceptions already noted, the outline is mostly clear, and in general the authors have succeeded in their goal of presenting a practical synthesis of the material found in the several excellent books in this field. The manual is highly and directly derivative, with liberal quotations from many sources, which has the obvious advantage of acquainting the reader with first-hand information that represents the current thinking of the profession.

[Reviewed by Thomas A. Seward in *Hisp*, 53 (September, 1970), 587-588; and by Catherine A. Maley in *MLJ*, 56 (February, 1972), 104-105.]

9. LADO, ROBERT

Linguistics across Cultures: Applied Linguistics for Language Teachers. Ann Arbor: The University of Michigan Press, 1957. ix + 141 pp.

This study is included in our survey for two reasons. First, it was one of the earliest comprehensive treatments of applied linguistics and language teaching and, second, most of the non-English examples are taken from Spanish. This book has been widely read and quoted by teachers and researchers alike. And though much of what Lado says here has been reexamined and modified, the easy-to-read study has earned a well-deserved popularity.

In Chapter 1 the author proposes the need for a systematic comparison of languages and cultures. His ideas were not new at the time, but he successfully calls attention to a coming together of linguistic and cultural components in teaching a FL. [For a fuller development of this notion, what Bull calls "linguistic organization of reality," see Nos. 5 and 6.]

Chapter 2 shows how the sound systems of two languages can be compared. Using mainly English and Spanish, Lado gives a familiar presentation of the phoneme, sound sequences, and pronunciation problems. He mentions, but hurries through, considerations of such topics as articulatory phonetics and dialect. Much more attention is given to the features of intonation.

In Chapter 3 the author discusses what grammar is and is not—for the user and the learner of a language. Also, prescription vs. description, form and meaning correlation, syntax, inflection, word classes, grammatical structure as a system of habits, and the application of contrastive analysis to the problems of teaching a FL. His structural-descriptive approach does not, of course, account for the speaker's language competence in terms of creative ability.

Vocabulary is studied in Chapter 4. The form, meaning, and distribution (rather than function) of words are discussed. No useful definition of the word emerges. The author also looks at cognates (true and false), idioms, how to classify words and how especially troublesome words can be presented to the learner.

In keeping with certain traditional emphases in language analysis and language learning, Lado devotes an entire chapter (5) to the comparison of writing systems. But the fact that he chooses to ignore the oral skills, understanding and speaking, weakens the possibilities for developing his final chapter on the comparison of two cultures. Nevertheless, culture, interpreted as the "ways of a people" and of which language is an important part, is viewed as a structured system of patterned behavior. The kind of model Lado suggests for analyzing cultures would reveal much of the information which has unfortunately but consistently been excluded from the FL classroom. Only in the last few years have teachers and textbook writers acknowledged with any success the possibility of presenting language as a cultural phenomenon. Lado has long been arguing for just such an approach.

Appended are various useful bibliographies, including one for specific languages.

[Reviewed by Albert H. Marckwardt in *LL*, 7:3-4 (1956-57), 135-137.]

10. MOLINA, HUBERT
      "The Learner, the Teacher, the Grammar and the Method in Designing an Instructional Program," *Hisp*, 54 (September, 1971), 439-444.

The author acknowledges three basic considerations which determine the nature and quality of any instructional program designed for teaching Spanish: the learner, the place of the program within the total school curriculum, and what we know about the teaching of Spanish. This last topic is discussed in order to make teachers aware of what to look for in the materials they choose, since the evaluation of materials is implicit in determining a FL program.

Some of Molina's premises: It is unreasonable to expect the learner to acquire all of the FL, since even a native speaker falls short of such mastery. It would be impossible and impractical to attempt to include in a pedagogical grammar all of the rules for the target language. Indeed, we do not even possess a complete inventory of rules for any language. And even if we did, classroom limitations of time would preclude the use of all the known rules. Needed is a careful selection of the lexicon and meanings of words which meet the specific communication requirements of the learner. Since no pedagogical grammar can provide all the information the FL learner must have, the materials writer should base his selections on valid criteria, such as frequency and other communication requirements. (The author suggests a list of "indispensable categories" of high frequency. Though few would quarrel with these categories, the list is too imprecise—e.g., "some transformational rules"—and the matter of hierarchy determining the interrelationships of these language classes must be discovered.)

A Learner's Dialect should be taught, which would serve as a framework to be expanded at higher levels. This implies control of the basics of a standard syntax and phonemic system. On the lexical level, the learner must be equipped only with an inventory of general terminology, which he will expand in two ways; one, by adding new words and two, by learning new meanings for the words he already knows. Cover terms should be stressed instead of specialized vocabulary, at least until the student has real need for the latter.

Molina continues his description of the learner's growing language competency by discussing various strategies to be employed for expanding the lexicon. These include, among other things, identification of members of lexical "sets" and being able to ask the right kinds of questions to elicit vocabulary examples and explanations. The author stresses that rote memorization should be minimized, since it does not reveal how the language system works. The Spanish verb *tener* is used to demonstrate how uneconomical any attempt to memorize its various functions can be, when the verb's role in the total language's operation is ignored.

The author's suggestion that the learner can come to know the meanings of parts of "true idioms" by uncovering their historical bases could produce false hopes, for in truth such keys to idiomatic usage are significantly rare. Better strategies are available to assist the student in acquiring necessary ease of idiomatic expression.

Though this article contains several sound reminders of requirements and limitations of the ideal pedagogical grammar, little if anything is new here, and the ideas are presented in a curious and awkward paragraph sequence.

11. POLITZER, ROBERT L. and CHARLES N. STAUBACH
   Teaching Spanish: A Linguistic Orientation. Boston: Ginn and Company, 1961. iii + 136 pp.

One of the earlier studies [See also No. 7] treating exclusively and rather comprehensively the role of applied linguistics in the teaching of Spanish. A companion volume modeled on *Teaching French* (1960), also by Politzer. The primary concern of this short manual is the use of linguistic analysis and its findings in the teaching of the basic skills at the high school and college levels. In their "Foreword," the authors tell us that their intention—for the most part carried out—is to place primary emphasis on the "application" aspect of linguistics and FL teaching, always with an eye toward practical approaches to concrete problems.

Part I of the book (Chapters 1 through 4) is devoted entirely to general methodological considerations: the meaning of "applied linguistics;" what is meant by a "linguistic" teaching method; some of the psychological aspects of language learning (the weakest section); and linguistic and non-linguistic teaching procedures. The primary interest or value in reading these pages from Part I today lies in the historical perspective one gets. Though unconventional and even "revolutionary" for many a teacher of Spanish at the time this book appeared, the ideas espoused strike us now as obvious, established (i.e., not "New Key" any more), or questionable—but questionable for some reasons different from those expressed during the first years of the past decade. On the other hand, much of what the authors offer as fact or advice holds firm for us today: "There is, or at least there ought to be, a very intimate relationship between linguistics . . . and language teaching." "The major contribution [of linguistics to teaching] lies in the systematic comparison of English and Spanish and the application of a teaching methodology . . . ." These, along with such notions as economy of presentation, the primacy of the oral aspect of language, the "units" of the language to be taught, in general, the planning and presentation of teaching material.

We are told that "linguists emphasize that language is behavior . . ." (2), but it must be pointed out that the authors discuss and analyze linguistic behavior throughout their book mainly as segmented performance rather than actual communication. But they do their best to make clear that linguistics or applied linguistics as such has no answer to many of the problems confronting the FL teacher. Their cautions, however, concern such matters as overcrowded classrooms, students with widely varying intelligence and aptitudes, motivation and attitudes, etc., rather than a consideration of the best way or ways to teach/learn linguistic competence, even if limited in terms of the total expressive potential of a language.

The emphasis here, then, is on systematic comparison (contrastive analysis) of the native and target languages and on drills designed to build up the "student's knowledge of the structure of the foreign language." The approach taken can perhaps best be characterized as viewing FL learning as learning language constructions which are building stones: "The student must . . . realize how [a] construction is 'made up,' how it 'comes apart,' how some building stones can be replaced by others." (5)

The question of traditional grammar, the direct method school of FL teaching, explicit or implicit use of grammar rules or analysis by the student—these are some of the central considerations dealt with, and superficially, in Part I. Typical declarations such as: "The actual learning of a foreign language takes place primarily by performance and habit-formation on the part of the student" (10) are viewed today as either overstatement or misstatement. And Chapter 4, the longest section of the first Part, establishes through example what is now understood to be the basic differences between "linguistic" and "non-linguistic" procedures in FL teaching, with contrastive analysis the key factor.

Although most of the pattern drill types known and used today are presented here, the treatment is by no means complete.

In Part II (beginning with Chapter 5) the structure of Spanish is introduced: first, phonetics and phonemics, then morphology and syntax, and for the most part as applied linguistics. The necessary linguistic terminology and concepts are established, but the authors couch practically the whole of their linguistic presentation in terms of pedagogical implications. Anyone familiar with phonetic studies today, and those for Spanish in particular, will note many symbols which have since been replaced by others—making for a much needed uniformity not characteristic of linguistic descriptions in general prior to 1960 and somewhat thereafter.

The teacher is given some very useful suggestions on how best (even experimentally) to teach some of the more knotty phonetic problem areas in Spanish. The authors, uncharacteristic of the writers of the day in this field, acknowledge the fact that learning problems vary from teacher to teacher and from student to student and that often no reliable rule of thumb is available.

Minimal and inadequate is the discussion of intonation and the various signal functions of the non-segmental features of Spanish phonology.

Given the limited space, the authors can do no more than outline in skeletal fashion morphology and how to teach it (Chapter 7). In particular the teacher will need more information on the Spanish noun and the verb system. [The reader is especially referred to Nos. 5 and 70.] However, most of the basic morphological classes are demonstrated for the verb, and the student or the teacher will at least be made aware of the difficulties involved in arriving at any adequate analysis for the Spanish verbal system. Particularly weak is the small section (88) on "Word Derivation."

Syntax is treated for the most part in terms of constituent analysis ("Noun and Verb Clusters," "The Position of . . . ," etc.), but it is arguable that this is at least one of the best ways to teach some of the basic grammatical patterns of Spanish. The majority of syntax patterns to be found in the typical first-year grammar are dealt with; though, importantly, some kernel constructions (for example those involving the different verb categories, or the with-verb pronouns) are not described. And one should question this statement: "The details of procedure and relative merits of these methods [of approaching the syntactical analysis of a language] are relatively unimportant to the Spanish teacher" (89). Further, the implications of the prediction that "the transformation approach opens up the possibility of teaching the entire system of syntax in a language through transformation exercises" (90) are hardly clearer today than when this study appeared.

Early in their study the authors tell us that words should not be taught in isolation. In a concluding chapter on teaching vocabulary the teacher is given useful insights as to the possibilities for teaching cognates (deceptive and real), synonyms, idioms, etc. The subtle and mostly unknown syntactic properties of words are not discussed, and the writers do not say enough about lexical selection, or appropriateness. Lexical difficulties are properly discussed in terms of the types of language-learning interference produced by the various lexical (class) correspondencies and divergencies that exist for English and Spanish. A final point regarding vocabulary is well made; namely, that after the first 750 to 1000 most common words (including the structural words) there is actually no validity in further rankings, since no absolute criteria can be established. Most textbook writers of today know this to be the case.

A short final chapter ("Conclusion") on the cultural and literary context for FL teaching is meant to give the teacher some practical guidelines for determining the best course content. Language is discussed as the mainstay, the key to a culture, and perhaps its most central element. The point the authors make is that whatever FL materials the teacher chooses, they should accurately reflect the culture whose language is being taught.

It is interesting to go through the useful appended bibliography in that the reader can see which linguistic studies—both general and for Spanish—influenced the approach taken in this manual. It is equally as interesting to take note of the items which do not appear in the bibliography, mainly because they have apeared since 1960. A mental weighing of what is "missing," along with a consideration of the important points made in this study to which teachers no longer adhere attests to the considerable research (if not real progress) that has been realized during the past decade.

[A revised edition, New York: Blaisdell Publishing Co., 1965, 198 pp., substantially unchanged from this original edition, is reviewed by Stanley M. Tsuzaki in *Hisp*, 49 (September, 1966), 553-554; and by Ann Tukey in *LL*, 16:3-4 (1966), 236-240. See also Donald D. Walsh's review of the first edition in *Hisp*, 45 (March, 1962), 162-163.]

12. SAPORTA, SOL

"Applied Linguistics and Generative Grammar," in *Trends in Language Teaching*, edited by Albert Valdman. New York: McGraw-Hill, 1966, 81-92.

This rather short but excellent article investigates the application of linguistics to the teaching of foreign languages, with particular attention paid to the possibilities and limitations of converting the linguist's scientific grammar into the teacher's pedagogical grammar. Though the author cites examples from English in making his points, he does include some examples from Spanish.

The reader is reminded that the specific forms teaching materials should take, if they are to be effective, must be determined by the basic assumptions regarding the nature of learning in general, i.e., extra-linguistic principles. The sad truth is, however, that we possess no adequate knowledge of the learning process which might enable us, for example, to decide on the superiority of adhering to the inductive or the deductive approach, or a combination of the two.

Saporta correctly points out that, by and large, descriptive linguistics of the forties and fifties somehow led textbook writers and users to stress the form, rather than the content, of teaching grammars, with only phonology receiving its due. This meant, in essence, that almost exclusive emphasis was on the "how" of FL teaching, rather than on the "what." This development is explained by Saporta as an understandable and inflexible adaptation of the behavioristic ("stimulus-response") learning theory so widely accepted at the time.

Turning to the impact that generative grammar subsequently had in bringing into question the nature of linguistic competence expected of our students and, indeed, the feasibility of attaining it, Saporta cites the kinds of native-speaker abilities we all possess: to distinguish between grammatical and ungrammatical sentences; to produce and understand an infinite number of acceptable utterances; to recognize ambiguous sentences and understand the interrelation of sentences. Almost parenthetically we are told that an examination of these abilities does not provide answers as to how they are acquired, though, according to Saporta, generative grammar makes clear the ways in which these capacities are unlikely to be acquired. He is, of course, referring to the specious role played by analogy function and repeated imitation of models, which does not involve actual creating of novel sentences by the FL learner.

Several of Saporta's assumptions are open to question. For example, the validity of his insistence that one is unable to arrive at some degree of competence through exposure and practice of sample forms and sentences. Or that any significant number of researchers or teachers actually believe that the total meaning of sentences is derivable from observation of the situations in which they occur (rather than an understanding of the structured language signal segments). On the other hand, he is quite correct in judging all pedagogical grammars as incomplete in establishing all the necessary grammatical and semantic distinctions which would be needed to allow internalization of those rules necessary for native performance. But it may well be the case that Saporta is requiring too much. In addition to conceding the mysteries of sentence recognition, he could have also considered the matter of teaching-learning limitations that in very real ways preclude acquisition of a second language (at least by post-adolescents), regardless of how he would have us convert even perfected scientific grammars of the future into implementable pedagogical materials.

Saporta is telling us that until the applied linguist has adequate knowledge of the explicit form, content, and "alleged" pedagogical function of such (abstract rule) formulations, he cannot hope to offer materials or methods for satisfactory second-language learning. It will likely come as no future shock that in arriving at this longed-for formula, the crucial pedagogical key is the latter element, and thus the linguist will have played but a corrective and peripheral role.

The author blames many of his colleagues for promising a panacea for the FL teacher predicated on the answers to be derived from the insights of generative grammar. Saporta makes it clear that he does not want to be included in this careless, misguided group.

Saporta will disturb and irritate many of his readers when he all but denies the primacy of the oral aspect of language and goes on to question that speaking a second language facilitates writing more than the reverse. ("Evidence seems to be largely anecdotal"— 85.) Close observation of the admittedly small but growing body of proof which valid experiments have afforded us conclusively shows that, at least for the more commonly taught languages in the U.S., the student who acquires the ability to speak the FL first, with little or no reliance on written material, has much less difficulty in transferring this oral skill to written form than vice versa. When both skills are sought, and with the terminal behavior judged in terms of economy, the learner stands a better chance of FL mastery if he accepts the temporary frustrations of initial avoidance of dependency on the written word. The weighted oral vs. written work, after initial exposure to the FL, is, of course, another question.

Additional interesting points raised by Saporta include the matter of storing memorized language segments vs. language as a rule-governed process. In this connection the author is not only painting in blacks and whites, but incorrectly characterizing the "linguistic method [with] memorization, pattern-practice exercises, and grammar by induction" (86), as simplistically equating learning a language with mere storing of a number of sentences.

Other notions investigated here include the familiar paradox in second-language learning, where conscious learning (internalizing) of rules interferes with performance, and the claims involved in the role of contrastive analysis.

Saporta concludes his excellent, provocative article by stating that the main contribution of generative grammar to FL teaching is that of providing the most meaningful statements about what (not how) is to be taught. Most language teachers will find distressing the fact that most of what the author clarifies is offered as proof of what we must but do *not* know about the nature of our task. But in moving forward in search of the necessary answers we cannot afford the kinds of false assumptions accepted by many teachers and no small number of linguists.

13. WOLFE, DAVID L.
   "Some Theoretical Aspects of Language Learning and Language Teaching," *LL*, 17 (December, 1967), 173-188.

First discusses the nature of language acquisition, distinguishing between the natural, unconscious process the child goes through in attaining linguistic puberty and, completing the learning cycle, the conscious learning of a FL by an adult. Adults cannot learn a language in the street, and children cannot learn one artificially, Wolfe tells us. But the fact that adults must acquire a second language artificially is no excuse, the author feels, for many practices common to FL teaching today. He is referring specifically to distorting the nature of language, forcing the student to lie. Structure drills (mainly item substitution) are shown to contain untrue statements, certainly not linguistic communication. The drill sentence should, then, allow the learner to express himself semantically as well as syntactically. The author's reasonable plea is for the teacher to use and encourage only language which reflects real events inside and outside the classroom.

Wolfe will have less success in converting the reader to his second point; namely, that since there is no originality or creativity in the technique of memorized dialogs, not even any real production of speech, the drill sentence is to be preferred. Another weak area in most classes, according to the author, is the teacher's failure to distinguish between concrete and abstract sentences in drills. Translation is not needed for the former, but necessary for the latter. If artificial language is to be avoided, and the native language not allowed to interfere, only sentences of the lowest level of concreteness should be practiced.

Though Wolfe seems to accept the theory that contrastive analysis can reveal a hierarchy of learning difficulties, he emphasizes the importance of language conflicts which do not originate in the native language. And for many students, automatic transfer is not all that difficult to avoid; in fact, they can fix on categories of difference and even invent some of their own. This is often a matter of study and practive habits. The question is not, says Wolfe, how to say "play" in English, but how to use *tocar, tomar* and *jugar* in Spanish. On the other hand, he overstates the solution to a *ser/estar*-like problem, which he sees as disappearing when adequately drilled.

As minimal stages required in the teaching of a FL to adults, these are discussed: 1) selection and ordering of linguistic units; 2) focus of attention on the units; 3) pronunciation of each item drilled; 4) vitalization; 5) sufficient repetition; 6) forced transfer of attention from structural form to general meaning; 7) creative use of the linguistic unit in original dialogs; 8) contrast drills; and 9) creative contrastive use of the linguistic unit in original dialogs. (This last step differs from 7 in that it is free conversation; the linguistic unit is no longer separated from the language whole.)

The real challenge for the teacher is "vitalization," through which the material is demonstrated, made clear, integrated, and comes alive. Teachers who are masters of this art should sit down together and share these insights in the form of an instructor's manual.

II. Teaching Phonology

14. BARRUTIA, RICHARD

"From Phoneme to Grapheme Audio-lingually," *Hisp*, 47 (December, 1964), 786-788.

Studies the question of when and how the audiolingual student can begin to read the foreign language with minimum difficulty. If the teacher has done his job well, the student will have half-mastered this next step by the time he is asked to read. The author suggests using memorized segments to practice and test spellings not predictable from the sounds. "Reading" orally memorized dialogs is not actually reading, but this kind of practice readies the student for his first reading experiences.

The student can begin writing by first copying prelearned material. The same technique used to develop the oral skills can be used to cue visual recall and develop the writing skill. Hints are given on how to lead the student, step by step, in controlled writing practice, but with an ever diminishing cue.

Contains a suggested list of twenty-three exercises in bridging the gap between oral and written work—all based on practice (not rules) to develop language habits.

15. BARRUTIA, RICHARD

"Visual Phonetics," *MLJ*, 54 (November, 1970), 482-486.

Develops a visual scheme for the presentation of the phonemic system of Spanish. Uses a series of diagrams designed to serve as practical aids for the student, as he comes to understand the considerable number of distinctive features for the sounds of Spanish and their relationship to the mechanisms of speech.

Barrutia follows Robert A. Hall's suggested prismatic constructions for establishing the Spanish consonant phonemes, but takes his own pedagogical approach a few important steps further. Emphasis on all Spanish sounds, necessitating a more complicated prismatic arrangement, but one which affords the learner with a full picture of the voiced/voiceless, point and manner of articulation. The suggested prisms, drawn within a detailed buccal cavity, focus the student's attention on the three "edges" of the diagrams, which constitute the various sound sets. Thus, the teacher can draw attention to alternating voiced and voiceless rows of stops, affricates, laterals, etc. Further, as the student moves from front to back, or vice versa, he pays attention to the specific points of articulation and the location (and position) of the articulators. The author incorporates into his inventory the nasal phonemes, by using a panel extended into the nasal cavity and joined at the appropriate points of the oral prism.

Suggested is the use of some color-coding in order to neatly separate different functions or modes. Either the blackboard or transparencies can be easily used in this way.

In a separate figure, Barrutia superimposes the familiar vowel quadrangle in that large and blank area (between the palatal and velar regions) not used by the consonants. The back vowels are represented as rounded by small circles along the quadrangle and an oval shape protruding from the lips. Were it not for the orderly presentation of the contrastive phonological features of Spanish, the final, complete diagram might seem a bit cluttered and confusing. But if the student grasps each bit of information in successive and meaningful steps, including actual articulation, he is not likely to be confused. Indeed, important clarifications should result from this clever presentation, for it not only yields a total inventory of Spanish phonemes, but also perfectly relates each sound to the basic criteria needed to deal with applied and theoretical phonetics.

Barrutia tells us that his own students invariably become excited about this illustrative approach to phonology, rather than consider it the dull and uninspiring lesson that it can be and so often is.

The principal effect this aid has is to allow the student to see and feel movement in speech as a *continuum* [*sic*] of change, rather than a series of fixed though sequential positions. Individualized and independent practice is made possible by this approach. Allophones, of course, must be treated mostly in other ways.

16. BEBERFALL, LESTER
    "*Y* and *LL* in Relaxed Spanish Speech," *Hisp*, 44 (September, 1961), 505-509.

Describes the occurrence of Spanish [ǰ], the voiced palatal affricate (referred to as "gio" by the author), which is said to have "no official standing in the Spanish language." Beberfall affirms the prevalence of this consonant sound in the Spanish of Latin America and, as confirmed in a letter held by the author from R. Menéndez Pidal, Spain as well. The author actually exaggerates what the Spanish linguist writes about [ǰ] and never clarifies its phonological status in the speech of Latin Americans.

Indeed, most of what Beberfall has to say about this sound is said in all too imprecise terms and based on questionable evidence, mainly from the Spanish of Texas Mexicans. Certain historical changes are cited in apparent support of a tendency to render /y/ as [ǰ], but the connections are vague. The only pattern that is more or less spelled out (/y/ = *y*, not *ll*, > [ǰ]) is explained in terms of a speaker's being conscious of the orhography. Certainly this is not the case. Patterns of distribution can be established for the dialect of Spanish (or that of Argentina) providing the author's examples and for grapheme correspondencies for [y], [ǰ], and [ž] – [See No. 5] – but this article does not contain the information.

In short, this article treats a very interesting phonological question, but no necessary synthesis is made of the sporadic bits of phonetic information.

17. BEYM, RICHARD
   "Practical Phonological Orientation for Effective Spoken Spanish," *Hisp*, 43 (March, 1960), 67-69.

American FL teaching methods are seen as less than consistently effective because the teacher has failed to create a learning situation which provides these elements, common to first-language acquisition: 1) Desire to participate in the culture; 2) High contact hours; 3) Merciless correction; 4) Memory and repetition; and 5) Effective practice and usage.

The author's basic premise is that, within the above framework, the "phonological level of speech" can be used profitably to teach spoken language effectiveness. This level is meant to include a command of the phonological segments of the language, including the allophones.

Beym emphasizes the importance of the student's increasing ability to recognize contrastive phonological patterns, which often come across as foreign noise to the beginner. Special attention needs to be given to sound duration and syllable make-up. The author perhaps exaggerates the basic difference between the flow of English and Spanish speech, the former with predominantly "glide bridges" between syllables, the latter, staccato-like rhythm. But he is correct in describing the beginner's habits, his initial inability to discriminate between the new sounds.

Several useful drills are suggested to help overcome interference and systematically learn the new sound system for Spanish.

The author appears not to be referring to allophones when he states: "It is at the level of phonemics that the learner of the second language most often produces what may be called something other than normal pronunciation." For he goes on to exemplify trouble areas involving transfer of English phonemes into the most obviously vulnerable phonological slots of Spanish. Complementary distribution drills for consonantal allophones are mentioned.

Though Beym doesn't actually spell out the different ways incorrect phonology can interfere with learning grammar, he at least hints at the possibility. Mention is also made of the importance of teaching the principal types of intonation patterns, with emphasis on hearing, imitation, and drilling. No one will deny that the more accurate the student is in controlling the FL's phonology, the more easily he can grasp its grammar. It would be most interesting to acquire some exact figures establishing the degree of this correlation.

18. BOGGS, RALPH S.
    Spanish Pronunciation Exercises. New York: Latin American Institute Press, Inc., 1954. 79 pp.

A concise drillbook-manual with intensive exercises for rapid improvement and mastery of oral Spanish and for speech correction. Intended also as an aid for native Spanish speakers "who wish to overcome defective speech habits," in phonological description and general approach, this booklet falls only slightly short of being prescriptive, and even presents some sounds not likely found in either Latin American or Iberian Spanish. For example, the second vowel sound the student is asked to practice is open [í] (4), supposedly found in a syllable closed by a consonant or preceded or followed by *rr* (*bis*, *ri*, etc.). Apart from being a questionable Spanish sound, in contrast to the familiar closed [í] [*sic*], this distinction creates a significant learning obstacle for the student. Intead of ridding his nonnative Spanish of intrusive English [ɪ], the student, in focusing on Mr. Boggs' [ì], might well transfer and affirm the English sound for Spanish [i]. Parallel, and equally specious and dangerous, are the author's close and open [ú] and [ù]. In citing these vowel qualities Mr. Boggs probably had in mind similar distinctions maintained in several early studies of peninsular Spanish pohonology. Particularly weak, incomplete and even confusing is the presentation of the occurrence of semivowels and semiconsonants in Spanish. The learner will need more adequate inventories and combinatory potentials for these frequent sounds.

    The vowels are presented first, then the consonants. Emphasis is on careful articulation of the individual sounds, and some, if not all of the controlling phonetic environments are established for the sounds to be practiced. The Spanish sound is always described in terms of its English counterpart or near-equivalent. (For Spanish–[éu̯]–represented *-uu-* : "Pronounce the *w* of English *now*, closing up the glide to end at the close position of *ú.*") These articulation descriptions and hints, telling the learner what to do with his tongue, mouth, etc., are followed, for each individual sound, by: 1) a few words containing the identified sound; 2) columns of words containing the sound under different environmental conditions; 3) words containing the sound grouped with words containing a different but similar sound with which it might be confused; 4) Spanish

proverbs which contain the sound (to be memorized); 5) a series of
sentences containing the words with the sound; 6) a conversation or dialog
between two persons whose speech is contrived so as to repeat many times
the sound that is being drilled; and 7) a review exercise, usually an
anecdote, a ballad, a tonguetwister, etc.

One might wish that the sample sentences be more colloquial, with
real-life utterances in place of some of the more studied prose passages.
The learner could probably profit more from better drills than from such
literary selections as the poetry of Bécquer, Lope de Vega, the *Cid*, etc.
There is no good reason why the student cannot absorb a bit of literary
heritage by way of phonological practice, but too often in the past we
have asked our students to imitate such models when instead they could
have and should have been listening to and imitating the everyday speech
of native speakers. "Imitating" the mellifluous sounds of Bécquer's poetry
as phonetic practice is not quite the same as performing similar exercises in
grammar practice, with literary masters serving only as guidelines.

In addition to the features already noted, the book also contains review
exercises and sound and spelling variant charts. The student who is already
familiar with the phonetics of Spanish and English in general will be only
slightly or momentarily puzzled by some of the atypical signs (e.g. [b] for
[ƀ], [ç] for [θ], [ii] for any Spanish vowel combination with semivowel
[i], etc.).

19. BOWEN, J. DONALD and ROBERT P. STOCKWELL
Patterns of Spanish Pronunciation: A Drillbook. Chicago:
University of Chicago Press, 1960. x + 137 pp.

It would be difficult to overestimate the influence this drillbook has
had on phonological studies after 1960. This is due to the fact that it was
one of the first full treatments of Spanish phonology based on the
precepts of structural linguistics and emphasizing the methods of
contrastive analysis. Though much of the material found in the study is
reiterated in another of the authors' well-known books, a volume of the
University of Chicago Contrastive Study Series [See No. 35], many of the
drills are to be found only in this earlier work. It is interesting to note
some differences in the analyses, etc. (for the most part minor in
importance), put forth in the different texts.

As the title indicates, this book deals principally with the problems
English speakers have in pronouncing Spanish. The various exercises and
the phonological analyses on which they are based were developed while
the authors were members of the linguistic staff of the School of
Languages of the Foreign Service Institute, and the results reflect the

information garnered during six years of experimentation with the teaching of pronunciation in large-scale intensive language programs. The authors' correct premise is that if the American learner is to develop a satisfactory pronunciation of Spanish, he must first learn to hear and imitate sounds new to him, ignore the differences between several sounds that are completely familiar to him, and then modify his manner of making most of the other sounds that are familiar to him. Implicit also in this aproach is the necessity of focusing on the comparative phonological features of the Spanish sound and its closest counterpart in the sound system of English. First, to hear and recognize; then to understand *how* the Spanish sound is different from the one the student should be making and reduce this understanding to the level of habit response.

The minimal-pair technique is the core operant employed in having the learner imitate the appropriate phonological segments. The authors feel that this is the best means of forcing the student to focus on a central, controlled problem in which interference (or transfer) is obvious. The materials are arranged to highlight the points of difficulty, and a quite adequate set of respelling symbols—neither phonetic nor phonemic, but a pedagogical tool—is used as an aid in listening.

Since the only objective of the drills is pronunciation, and, thus, the meaning of the utterances is of no or minimal importance, no distracting translations are given. The student is told to consider the sequences like nonsense imitations of what actual speakers of Spanish could use and might use (with each member of the minimal pair with its own different meaning).

In addition to good descriptions of and drills for the various intonational patterns (often referred to as the stepchild of the Spanish classroom), the book presents:

1. Notes about the differences between the comparable sounds of each language.
2. Descriptions of the articulation of Spanish sounds not present in English.
3. The problems arranged in a hierarchy of importance from most important to least important.
4. A respelling of Spanish that symbolizes consistently each problematic detail.
5. Lists of items that illustrate the distribution of the sounds.
6. Extensive examples for classroom drill on all the problems, each drill arranged to focus attention on the specific problem it is designed to help the student overcome.

The drillbook has on the whole an admirable arrangement, leading the student through successively more difficult and crucial material. First there is a brief, if oversimplified, introduction to the basic elements of intonation. This is followed by a treatment of the vowels (including a fine presentation of the complex nuclei), then the consonants, and finally an expanded summary chapter on intonation. It would be difficult to agree with the transcribed analyses for all the given English and Spanish sentences, but in the main the presentation is clear and orderly, with remarkably few errors.

[Reviewed by Sol Saporta in *Hisp*, 44 (September, 1961), 575-576.]

20. BOWEN, J. DONALD
    "Teaching Spanish Diphthongs," *Hisp*, 46 (December, 1963), 795-799.

Suggests the possibility that the clarity and apparent simplicity claimed by the Spanish orthographic system can often mislead the student. The author's specific reference is to the diphthongs, the analysis and pedagogical presentation of which have been regularly debated among linguists and teachers of Spanish.

Bowen begins his presentation of the issue and his own solutions by showing how part of the basic problem is created by use of the same letter to represent both a vowel and a consonant. The author rejects the traditional analysis which accounts for the overlap (/i, y/, /u, w/) by dividing the Spanish vowels into two groups: strong and weak vowels. Bowen believes that the concept "weak/strong" is both feeble and misleading, in that there is no consistency of identify or phonetic distribution. But to insist that /i/ and /u/ are inherently weak is not the only alternative to a reclassification of these sounds according to their appearance in the syllable.

In place of the traditional explanation of the Spanish diphthongs, Bowen suggests two concepts which he sees as "both linguistically defensible and pedagogically useful." The first of these is the identity of a semivowel (a transition sound between that of vowel and consonant), which is determined by syllable structure and stress pattern. The second concept concerns the function of the semivowel in syllable structure. Bowen prefers to consider the onglides /y/ and /w/ consonantal, but part of a complex vowel nucleus when offglides. The author concedes that /y/ and /w/, when the second or third member of a consonant cluster, are difficult to justify as consonants, because of the lack of consonantal quality. To do so means allowing three-consonant clusters (e.g., *pliego* = /ply-/), which is viewed here as the best linguistic solution and an improved pedagogical approach. This is not clearly the case. Rather unconvincing also is Bowen's conclusion that the three-consonant analysis explains the "enormous difficulty" students have with words like *pliego*, *clueca*, etc., while they experience no difficulty with the sequences /pl-, kl-/ + vowel. Regardless of phonemic identity, Spanish [plie-] will be troublesome for speakers of English simply because no such sequence of sounds exists in their native language.

Classifying semivowels as distinct from vowels and including them in diphthongs only when they follow a vowel may have the advantages (simplicity and usefulness) Bowen avers—certainly as regards phonetic/ phonemic transcription. But, as the author acknowledges, it is certainly arguable that both a spelling and a phonemic transcription are warranted for Spanish. For, considering the diphthong situations as separate problems or the Spanish sound system as a whole, there is so much redundancy that any kind of respelling would seem to have limited consequences. Besides, many teachers find that the semivowel/ semiconsonant values tend to take care of themselves when they receive adequate emphasis in the early learning stages.

21. CÁRDENAS, DANIEL N.
Introducción a una comparación fonológica del español y del inglés. Washington, D.C.: Center for Applied Linguistics, 1960. x + 63 pp.

Primarily a pedagogical treatment of the sound system of Spanish, including a systematic comparison of the native (English) and target languages. The author's intention is to reveal all of the important pronunciation problems, knowledge of which can fulfill this manual's three-fold purpose: "1) To serve as a point of departure for further scientific comparisons between English and Spanish as well as other languages; 2) To serve as a basis for the instruction of our Spanish teachers of tomorrow; and 3) To serve as a reference for the hundreds of present Spanish teachers who may not have found a solution to some of their pronunciation problems."

The first part of this study is a brief introduction to phonemics and the sounds of English and Spanish. The format and approach are much those of the descriptivists. (Cárdenas acknowledges especially the analyses of Trager and Smith for English, the earlier works of Stockwell, Bowen, and Silva-Fuenzalida for Spanish.) Though phonetic and phonemic theory is kept to a minimum, the author clearly establishes his terminology and provides good examples for his points. Articulatory phonetics is chosen as the descriptive framework because of its easy application in the teaching-learning situation. Economy of presentation is sacrificed, in that the segmental phonemes of Spanish are established twice—first, for

Spanish alone, and a second time for an English-Spanish comparison. Consonants are described first, then vowels, the syllable, and stress. No dialect or proto-system is identified, but most of the phonetic information would appear to be taken from Navarro Tomás [See No. 32], who is frequently cited.

Some elements of American Spanish are included in the section which compares English and Spanish sounds. The basic weakness here is the author's failure to bring out the important learning problems involving phonemic and phonetic transfer, which would include for example the English sounds /d/, /s/, /z/ and others. Cárdenas fares better in his presentation of consonant clusters and phenomena involving the syllable.

The third part of the manual, which constitutes almost one-half of its content, treats intonation. The exposition is involved but for the most part clear. Some of the contour patterns, even for basic utterance types, are not those given in the most recent studies. The author mainly follows Bowen (*Hisp*, 39, 1956, pp. 30-35) and Stockwell and Silva-Fuenzalida (*Lang*, 32, 1956, pp. 641-665) for the Spanish patterns.

A glossary of terms, a bibliography, and a set of sound charts and graphs conclude this volume.

[Reviewed by Charles W. Kreidler in *Hisp*, 44 (December, 1961), 770-771.]

22. CONTRERAS, HELES
   "Vowel Fusion in Spanish," *Hisp*, 52 (March, 1969), 60-62.

An account of vowel reduction and elision in the author's colloquial Chilean Spanish. Contreras studies three specific phenomena involving contiguous vowels; namely, 1) when a diphthong is formed or a vowel is lost: *casa humilde* [kàsaumílde ~ kàsumílde] ; 2) where there is fusion: *café helado* [kafèládo] ; and 3) when no fusion takes place: *casa alta* [kàsaálta] . (The phonetic transcription assumes a stress-adjustment rule which accounts for the secondary ['] stress.)

Stress, word boundaries, and vowel position are given as the determining factors. The different stress patterns for 1) and 2) above account for the different fate of the onset vowel, and in Contreras' dialect, at least, no fusion occurs because the first of the two adjacent vowels is unstressed. Word boundaries are distinct from morpheme boundaries, since the latter preclude either diphthongization or loss of the first vowel. Further, the optional vowel elision with two unstressed vowels does not occur when a front and a back vowel combine. And if the contiguous vowels differ in tongue height, and with the usual diphthongization conditions obtaining, the highest vowel becomes a glide. If there is no difference in stress or tongue height, the first vowel becomes a glide.

Contreras next writes four optional rules needed to account for his data. They are followed by reformulations and examples.

The author has found it helpful to specify to students the cases where vowels across word boundaries undergo no modification.

23. DALBOR, JOHN B.
   Spanish Pronunciation: Theory and Practice. New York: Holt, Rinehart and Winston, 1969. xi + 322 pp. Tapes are available.

A comprehensive introduction to Spanish phonetics and phonemics which serves primarily as a manual of oral drill for English speakers wishing to acquire an authentic Spanish accent. The text was pretested in Professor Dalbor's classes at the Pennsylvania State University.

While granting the possible theoretical superiority of generative phonology, the author bases his phonological analysis on the principles of structural-descriptive linguistics, since this latter approach is to be desired for pedagogical reasons. Thus, there is, for example, heavy reliance on the traditional point and manner of articulation presentation.

The variety of Spanish used is a normalized Latin American dialect ("General American Spanish"). Some important dialectal variations are discussed.

Traditional terminology is used throughout the text, along with the phonetic symbols one would find in Navarro Tomás [See No. 32]. The author does utilize some new terms of his own invention, especially as regards the Spanish vocalic nuclei, which are always troublesome to describe and learn and which are here nicely simplified.

Phonetic and phonemic transcriptions abound. Thus, the student is encouraged to practice and master, step by step, each phonological problem. The suprasegmental features of stress, pitch, and juncture are also fully treated.

The first six chapters are intended as an introduction to linguistics, with specific application to Spanish phonology. The next seventeen chapters are concerned with the consonants, the next nine vowels, the next five the suprasegmentals, the next one more general pronunciation problems, and the final one orthography.

Most chapters have the following format: 1) a list of the phonemes presented in the chapter; 2) a listing of the allophones; 3) facial diagrams; 4) articulatory descriptions; 5) examples of allophone distributions; 6) significant dialectal variations; 7) the principal contrasts between Spanish and corresponding English sounds likely to produce interference; 8) bibliographical references; 9) oral drills; 10) written exercises. Review chapters are also included.

Though the author believes that repetition is the "backbone" of learning, he incorporates many drills that go beyond the familiar minimal pair technique. Students are asked to answer questions, repeat phrases, and practice reading paragraphs. Contrasts of correct vs. incorrect forms are used, but the student is never asked to imitate an incorrect model. Aural discrimination drills precede repetition drills, i.e., perception precedes production. Most drills are for oral use in the lab and in the classroom.

The Appendix contains rules, charts and practice readings.

This excellent, carefully written manual is accompanied by a full tape program and a Teacher's Manual. The text will likely be widely used in college courses in Spanish phonology.

[Reviewed by Robert Phillips in *Hisp*, 52 (December, 1969), 975-976; and by Spurgeon Baldwin in *Hisp*, 55 (September, 1972), 612-613.]

24. DREHER, BARBARA and JAMES LARKINS
"Non-semantic Auditory Discrimination: Foundation for Second Language Learning," *MLJ*, 56 (April, 1972), 227-230.

Using a two-part non-semantic auditory discrimination tape, the authors tested forty first-year Spanish students at the college level. The hypothesis was that those subjectively prejudged good or poor in pronunciation by their teachers would score high or low, respectively, in this experiment.

Some efforts were taken to control the variables. The testees were limited to students of similar age and FL background.

Part I consisted of fifty paired nonsense English syllables, for which the student was to decide whether or not the two items sounded the same. In general the items progressed from gross to fine discriminations and from simple to complex phonological structure, with examples of those sounds identified as the most easily confused (Θ, đ, š, s, etc.). Part II tested the learner's ability to identify possible Spanish sound combinations in a list of fifty non-words.

One cannot be certain that these forty subjects represented a typical class segment, and in fact their teachers prejudged only seven total as poorest or best in pronunciation—the large majority falling in the middle range. The original 4-point ranking was actually collapsed to two.

The results held no surprises. Though the students more easily discriminated the paired nonsense syllables in English than they identified the Spanish sound sequences, the "good" group outperformed the "poor" group significantly. Statistical analyses showed that the student differences followed a pattern rather than occurred by chance.

All teachers of Spanish are familiar with the difficulties of rating oral production. If, as many researchers hold, accurate oral production requires accurate discrimination, then perhaps tests such as these and others can be perfected to isolate trouble areas as well as good and poor pronouncers. Used as diagnostic and aptitude indicators in the early stages or as achievement tests later on, the teacher would be better equipped to handle the phonological problems of his students.

25. ESTARELLAS, JUAN
   "Problems in Teaching Spanish Pronunciation and Writing by the Audio-lingual Method: A Case Study," *Hisp*, 55 (March, 1972), 96-98.

Taking some liberties in outlining the "principles" of the audiolingual method, Estarellas calls for a method which includes practice on phonemic-graphemic relationships from the start in FL study. In an attempt to evaluate the evidence, on the one hand, that exposure to the written word can inhibit free oral expression and, on the other, that graphic symbols can in fact aid in evoking oral responses, the author conducted an experiment involving high school students of Spanish.

The twofold purpose of the experiment was 1) to ascertain the typical phonological problems of audiolingual students and 2) to determine whether remedial work on phonemic-graphemic relationships would solve some of these problems. Diagnostic tests pinpointed the usual sound discrimination difficulties with the vowels, consonants, and intonation patterns. In writing, the tested students had particular problems in discriminating consonants (*qu, c, f, j, g, h, y, ll, s, z*). The greatest difficulty was with new words. In general the students were more successful in distinguishing between questions and statements.

For two months the students worked approximately twenty minutes a week with special materials designed to teach sound-letter relationships. Aural-phonemic and graphemic discrimination practice was followed by pronunciation. Work on syllabication, stress, linking, and intonation was also included.

The initial test was repeated after the two months and the mean score (of a possible 100) rose from 73 to 86. And the teachers noticed a general improvement in classroom performance in pronouncing and writing.

This interesting pilot project could be further developed and the results judged against other strategies for teaching the same information and skills.

26. ESTARELLAS, JUAN and TIMOTHY F. REGAN, JR.
    "Effects of Teaching Sounds as Letters Simultaneously at the
    Very Beginning of a Basic Foreign Language Course," *LL*, 16:3-4
    (1966), 173-182.

Results of an experiment designed to determine the effects of teaching
Spanish sounds and graphs simultaneously, rather than delaying
introduction of the written symbols. Finding only "mythical beliefs and
philosophies," rather than valid research evidence in support of the
generally accepted ordering of skill development (listening, speaking,
reading, writing), the authors wanted to substantiate their feeling that the
written word should be used as soon as possible. They recognize that
negative transfer from interfering orthography is real and inevitable, but
are convinced that the appropriate kind of teaching could minimize this
interference. They cite research claims which hold that visual cues aid both
memory and auditory discrimination.

Working under this assumption, a pilot project was begun at a Fort
Lauderdale, Florida high school, to find out "whether the teaching
simultaneously of sounds and letters at the beginning of a foreign-language
course helps or hinders the student's progress." Self-instructional
procedures [See No. 110], based on programed materials, were used by
the experimental group. It was felt that this approach lends itself better to
the teaching of phonemic and graphemic systems than the conventional
classroom/laboratory situation.

A control group and an experimental group of students, of similar
average I.Q. levels and age (13), were formed from a beginning Spanish
class of 40. The control (or regular) group began with tapes and classroom
work with the A-LM materials, laboratory sessions, but no text. The
experimental group was given written programed materials coordinated
with audio tape recordings prepared by the authors. This linear program
included problems in discrimination, pronunciation, and writing of the
Spanish phonemes, syllabication, stress, linking, and intonational patterns.
Some frames called for only written responses, others were both oral-aural
and written. Phonemes were associated with their letter transcription, and
then the graphemes were used for aural discrimination. Immediate
reinforcement followed for the phonemic-graphemic links.

Findings: At the end of about four weeks both groups were given tests
covering the problem areas stressed in the programed lessons (Writing,
Stress, Syllabication, Linking, Intonation, and Reading). Predictably, the
control group came out second best. Assuming no better than good
teaching for the classroom section, these students doubtless would have
tested superior to the experimental group in other FL competencies.

Some five weeks into the semester the experimental group had overtaken the others in learning dialogs and also slightly outperformed them on the first A-LM Listening Comprehension Test. The authors fail to make clear that all students spent the same amount of time at study and practice. And other variables preclude any conclusive claims. Certainly the limited scope of this experiment does not yield sufficient evidence that "it seems apparent that *all* four skills can successfully be taught at the same time." Furthermore, the authors' concept of operational phonemic-graphemic links is puzzling and very questionable.

27. GREEN, JERALD R.

Spanish Phonology for Teachers: A Programmed Introduction. Philadelphia: The Center for Curriculum Development, Inc., 1970. xiii + 131 pp.

This programed course in Spanish phonology—the first of its kind—is an expanded version of an experimental program with an original objective to teach and compare only the consonantal systems of Spanish and English. Later used in a graduate methods course for in-service teachers of Spanish taught by the author, *Spanish Phonology for Teachers* was revised and field-tested on several occasions, and its final form reflects both student and teacher responses. The intended audience is wide: the undergraduate Spanish major; the teacher-trainee; the student in a methods course; a person working on phonetics on his own; any Spanish teacher who recognizes the need to better his knowledge of the sound system of Spanish; and the department chairman, the language supervisor, or the teacher trainer who needs to acquire a systematic understanding of Spanish phonology, either as a review or an introduction to the topic.

The program consists of 750 carefully ordered frames. Student responses can either be written on separate sheets or directly in the program. Each page is divided into six frames, and when the student reaches the last page he merely returns to page 1 and proceeds through the program on the second row of frames. The confirmation or correct response is given in a square to the left of the succeeding frame and, therefore, the student can verify his answer before proceeding to the next item.

Most of the responses require short answers—usually one or two words or symbols. For the most part the "answers" can be found in preceding items, though worded differently. (Typical example: "In articulatory phonetics a phonetic transcription is usually transcribed between___." By the time this frame is given the student has already noticed that brackets are used to enclose phonetic information.) Many linguistic expressions are translated (in parentheses) into Spanish.

The subsections of the program: language and linguistics; phonetics and phonology; voicing; point of articulation; manner of articulation; consonant phonemes and allophones; dialectal variations; vowels, stress; vowel classifications; glides, diphthongs and triphthongs; rhythm; and intonation. A useful feature of the sequencing is intervening review frames, as well as a final review frame presenting a list of linguistic terminology and phonetic symbols. Also, a final examination is included at the end of the program.

Another good feature of this program is the use of blank charts for the Spanish vowels and consonants, which the student fills in as he teaches himself these phonemes and allophones.

The terminal objectives of the program are reasonable and attainable in that they follow from the progressive steps asked of the user. The procedural directions are clear and minimal, and the student should have few if any real difficulties in completing the program, for all he has to do is observe faithfully the numerical order of the frames. But perhaps a sound suggestion to the student might be that instead of merely flipping the page for the ready answer, without thinking, he should first focus on exactly what information (answer) is being established and endeavor to make a good guess based on what he has learned by that point in the program.

While this program teaches much information *about* Spanish phonology, the student does not actually practice it. The student will have to utilize a drillbook, preferably with a taped program [See Nos. 23 and 28] if he is to improve or master actual production of the sounds of Spanish.

The author delimits—perhaps to an unnecessary degree—his audience in stating that "the linguistic assumptions . . . require that the user have completed three to four years of secondary-level Spanish and several semesters of college Spanish [and be] a major in the language" (iv). And the program is not proffered as a substitute for the undergraduate course in Spanish phonetics.

Though the accuracy of certain statements can be questioned ("Spanish-speakers usually eliminate the [d] in words ending in -*ado*. . ."), in the main the information is quite accurate and clearly presented. Many especially highly motivated users will doubtless profit from this programed course.

[Reviewed by Roger Hadlich in *Hisp*, 54 (May, 1971), 408-409.]

28. HADLICH, ROGER L., JAMES S. HOLTON and MATÍAS MONTES
   A Drillbook of Spanish Pronunciation. New York: Harper and
   Row, Publishers, 1968. xviii + 236 pp. Available with tapes.

A drillbook and manual of Spanish phonetics and phonemics. This is a comprehensive study, more usable than materials that have been available to date. It has ample, good drills and also contains clear information of a descriptive and theoretical nature. The authors acknowledge their indebtedness in drawing upon well-known phonetics texts, but they have ably improved upon their models.

The teacher will find that this drillbook allows him maximum flexibility in editing the materials to his particular needs.

The drillbook is accompanied by a set of tapes containing all of the pronunciation exercises; thus the student can prepare himself for class by performing the drills in the language laboratory. The instructions and explanations are unusually clear and untechnical, and the student can work alone without procedural difficulties.

The basis for all the drills is the concept of contrastive analysis which reveals interference caused by the learner's unconscious habits.

For each of the thirty-four "Pronunciation Problems" there is a brief discussion followed by two types of exercises: 1) discrimination ("Listen and Compare," "Listen and Decide"), and 2) practice ("Listen and Repeat"). The repetition drills are generally short and simple, though they are graded and become successively more challenging, ending up with "internalization exercises."

In keeping with increasingly widespread practice, the authors have wisely elected to present their own version of normalized Latin American Spanish (their term is "general Spanish"). Some dialectal variations are described.

Some plus features not found in most similar or earlier texts: careful separation of sound and spelling; good treatment of the semivowels; full discussion of intonation; good drills on vowel length; the use of clear pictures to elicit phonetic segments.

Homogeneous groupings are not maintained, and certain linguistic concepts could perhaps be introduced earlier, but on the whole this is a solid, useful drillbook.

[Reviewed by William W. Cressey, *LL*, 18 (June, 1968), 141-142; and by H. J. Frey in *Hisp*, 52 (March, 1969), 177-179.]

29. HAMMERLY, HECTOR
   "And Then They Disbelieved Their Ears," *Hisp*, 53 (March, 1970), 72-75.

Results of an experiment in which the author wanted to gather empirical data to substantiate his impression that there is a high degree of interference from spelling when the student is asked to perform orally.

The subjects of the experiment were 35 college students selected at random with no background in Spanish, but who averaged 2.8 years of FL study. In order to ascertain orthographic interference the participants were asked to record ten Spanish utterances of two to four syllables each. They first recorded the oral model three times, with no written aid; then they recorded the native speaker's version twice as they read from the written words; next, they read the utterances (with no oral guide); lastly, after these three steps had been accomplished for all ten items, the students recorded their reading of the complete list.

The phonologic problem was limited to those areas of phonemic conflict for which divergent phonemic-graphemic correlations exist in Spanish and English. No phonetic, phonemic or graphemic elements unknown to the subjects were included. Cognate words were avoided, and in general the experimentor managed to control the significant variables.

Hammerly presents the results in a chart which shows the relative percentages for correct and incorrect sounds. For example, [z] was given for the /s/ of *zapato* by 54 percent of the students while they were reading the word along with the oral model, 74 percent, with only the spelling available, 94 percent at the final reading, again with no oral stimulus, but *never* (i.e., only /s/) at first try, imitating the oral model. Similar high degrees of negative transfer were found for *n + p, b,* and *v,* though *h* and *qu* fared better.

In general as soon as the written stimuli appeared the subjects "disbelieved their ears" and were guided by the spelling. For this reason, the author argues for a pre-reading period, or at least practice in transcription, to overcome the inevitable mistakes caused by sound-spelling correlations.

30. MATLUCK, JOSEPH L.
"The Presentation of Spanish Pronunciation in American Textbooks," *MLJ*, 41 (May, 1957), 219-228.

An assessment of the inaccuracies and weaknesses of the phonological presentations found in thirty grammars, with suggestions for methodological and factual improvement. Though many of the shortcomings gleaned from these texts have since been eliminated, some have not; and this article is of interest and importance as an historical statement of the distance and direction the teaching of the sounds of Spanish has traveled in the past twelve years.

Matluck's main objections to what he observes are that too many textbook treatments overstate and overuse English equivalents for the target sounds and do not pay enough attention to the nature of sound articulations. He disparages those who have played down phonetics on the excuse that it constitutes an introductory course of its own (or should) and usurps too much time. The author's proposal is that teachers should continue with some of the then current practices, but with certain revisions. These would include the use of English examples only when valid and helpful, and the teaching of the distinctive Spanish articulations and how they differ from similar English sounds. In general Matluck argues for taking advantage of the student's intellectual level and capacities. The learner should be held responsible for pronunciation, just as for the grammar. Furthermore, the topic must be developed throughout a course (or text), until an acceptable competence has been achieved. It is to be noted that most introductory textbooks now measure up to these stipulations.

The author reviews the principal problem areas in teaching Spanish phonology, citing some of the most frequent textbook practices and ways to improve them. He dislikes most of the English word examples and would eliminate certain distinctions, for example, close and open /e/ – [e] vs. [ẹ] . (Matluck would teach only the latter, in order to avoid confusion.) As for the consonants, he is offended the most by imprecise and misleading descriptions. He comes up with some really outrageous examples of how these sounds have been presented. No instant solutions are found for troublesome /r/ and /ř/, but the teacher is wisely cautioned to be on the lookout for vowel neutralization in a syllable closed by /r/.

Less attention is given to inaccuracies in the treatment of stress and to the ignored stepchild, intonation.

While Matluck overlooks some problems and purposefully avoids others (Spanish [s] vs. [z] , for example), he has called our attention to a serious matter, one which bears directly on how effectively textbooks serve both the teacher and the student.

31. MILLS, DOROTHY HURST
    "Why Learn Contrasting Intonation Contours?", *Hisp*, 52 (May, 1969), 256-258.

Describes the structure and use of a classroom chart intended as a visual aid in learning the correct intonation patterns of Spanish or English. The author defends the need for such charts on the basis of typical "pragmatic students who ask *why* at all levels of learning, . . . no longer content to learn something for the sheer joy of learning." These students are depicted as a chorus of "why"-askers, whose questions must be answered before they will "submit . . . to that tortuous process called *learning*."

Be this as it may, the intonation pattern chart has been used to motivate learning in answering the "why" questions which arise when intonation patterns are studied or practiced. The teacher must control all the contours, and the student has to develop a feel for those in his own language. This is arrived at through conscious practice in discriminating and producing. (Mills does not suggest that discrimination should precede production.)

Before the teacher presents the chart, the student runs through a three-step procedure: 1) He practices the patterns, paying particular attention to changes in stress and pitch (no mention is made of juncture); 2) He is made aware of contrasting patterns of English; and 3) He hums or whistles the contours presented by the teacher. The student is ready for the chart only after he attains conscious control of the English patterns.

The chart (a transparency, a wall chart or a sheet prepared for the opaque projector) contains side-by-side examples, with numbered descriptions (Engl. 231 vs. Span. 211, etc.), the English on the left, the Spanish on the right, with adjacent infix boxes for each which permit arrow drawings to demonstrate the contrasting pitch levels for the two languages. The segments of the chart are presented one by one, beginning with an English contour, which the teacher reads and explains. The students follow the arrow to the corresponding Spanish pattern of pitch levels, of a different sentence type, and thereby focus on the significant contrasts. The learner works his way through the principal patterns, beginning with the English statement of annoyance or disgust, then the uncolored one, next the question forms, and lastly the Spanish vocative contour, /111], which implies discourtesy or servility in English.

To be noted are a potentially dangerous oversimplification in the pattern descriptions and the omission of the juncture feature. Different versions of this kind of chart could of course be used at different stages in the learning.

32. NAVARRO TOMÁS, TOMÁS
Manual de pronunciación española. New York: Hafner Publishing Co., 5th ed., 1957. 336 pp.

First published in 1918, this remains the standard work on Spanish phonetics. Represents a lifetime dedicated to gathering and interpreting data on the sounds of Castilian Spanish. The purpose of this book is to facilitate the teaching of Spanish phonology. No attempt is made to enter into underlying theoretical questions, but instead every effort is made to present a complete inventory of those sounds which represent "correct Spanish pronunciation," or *"la que se usa corrientemente en Castilla en la conversación de las personas ilustradas."* Navarro further affirms that his descriptions are those of Castilian *"sin vulgarismo y culta sin afectación."* By "correct" the author intends simply "not vulgar," with an eye on the orthography. In short, Navarro's approach is as much prescriptive as it is descriptive and indeed those points which have been questioned concern this important fact. The text has never been revised in the light of modern phonological theory. These shortcomings have not, however, significantly reduced the usefulness of this volume or other studies by the famous Spanish phonetician, from whom others in the field have drawn heavily.

Though intended as a pedagogical tool, there is practically no resemblance between the format of this text and others [See Nos. 19, 23 and 28] intended for the same use. Instead, it has served as a source book, often used at the advanced (graduate) level. Because of its completeness, it has been for the investigator a reminder of the many areas of Spanish phonetics which either lack consensus or have required additional study.

The introduction to general phonetics covers the nature of sounds and their articulation. This careful description of how sounds are made and contrast with one another prepares the reader for the detailed descriptions which accompany the treatment of the phonetic values in subsequent chapters.

The vowels are analyzed first. Allophonic values are posited for each of the five vowels which would not be included in a classroom presentation. Examples of these variants would be: [i̹] *abierta* - *silba*; [i̞] *relajada* - *púlpito*; [ə] *relajada* - the second vowel of *húmedo*; etc. Though Navarro is not suggesting for this last vowel an articulation as central as schwa, the kind of vowel reduction involved here—and for the other vowel phonemes—is slight, subtle and has no bearing on distinctions to be made for the student. The semivocalic and semiconsonantal qualities of /i/ and /u/, yes, these are important; likewise, open [e̞] - [pa-pe̞l], [pe̞-r̝o] - in an open syllable and when before and after certain sounds. Open [o̞], supposedly found in environments similar to those of [e̞], has, after the diphthongs and triphthongs, been the value least agreed upon. While the sound was regularly included in earlier pedagogical treatments of Spanish phonetics, it does not appear in many of the more recent texts. In fact, authors have come to ignore or reject Navarro's 'relaxed' vowel allophones probably because they have at best only a dialectal reality and, more importantly for the learner, differ ever so slightly from (one of) the principal allophone(s) or else would needlessly trouble the student. Another theory is that these subtle variants will take care of themselves, since the Anglo tends to neutralize unstressed vowels anyway.

The consonants are familiarly handled, and good examples are given for each. The author also describes what hapens when words come together, thus creating new combinations of sounds. This is followed by a brief discussion of Spanish intonation. (Navarro's fuller treatment of this topic is his *Manual de entonación española*, 2nd ed. New York: Hispanic Institute, 1948.) Appended are exercises on articulation and intonation, and some useful phonetic transcriptions of selected materials.

[The 3rd edition, 1926, is reviewed by E. C. Hills in *Hisp*, 9 (December, 1926), 363-368.]

33. SACKS, NORMAN P.
"A Study in Spanish Pronunciation Errors," *Hisp*, 45 (May, 1962), 289-300.

Outlines the pronunciation problems found in the speech of twenty-nine participants in a 1961 NDEA Spanish Summer Language Institute at the University of Wisconsin. The study includes most if not all the common difficulties experienced by beginning FL students and many "mistakes" which either show up sporadically or are often overlooked by the instructor and the learner.

The data for this survey were taken from rather lengthy pre- and post-institute recordings of read dialogs and poems. The participants recorded the same material twice in order to ascertain the amount of progress made in the phonetics course. Drills and explanations for many of the errors were taken from *Modern Spanish* (Harcourt Brace, 1960) and Bowen and Stockwell's *Patterns of Spanish Pronunciation: A Drillbook* [See No. 19.] The author provided additional material as needed for those errors not studied in either of these sources.

Quite possibly some patterns of errors other than those taken from the tapes would have occurred, had the teachers recorded material they were not actually reading.

These are the principal areas of pronunciation difficulty, with accompanying suggestions for drill, found in the Spanish of most of the participants:

1) Intonation. All of the teachers demonstrated weaknesses in this area, especially with the question patterns. Too, many tended to use inappropriate stresses and pitches which were too high.

2) Minimal vowel contrasts under weak stress. As Sacks points out, perhaps the most striking example of the influence of English speech habits upon Spanish (and surely one of the most difficult problems). Following Stockwell and Bowen, the author had the teachers perform considerable practice with minimal pairs.

3) Fusion or modification of adjacent vowels across word boundaries. The participants, like beginners, resisted fusing especially two identical

contiguous vowels. Other similar difficulties involved word boundary situations which the teachers did not know. Sacks wonders if the dictation exercise perhaps influences certain learners to respect only written boundaries for fear of making written mistakes.

4) Modification of consonants across word boundaries. The two principal phenomena of assimilation (the phonemes /n/ and /s/ and frication (/b,d,g/). Predictably the participants' errors were found mostly across word boundaries, rather than in word-internal position. In general, those who failed, for example, to voice /s/ to [z] in *desde* also ignored the voicing in *nos dio.* Similar patterns for the various allophones of /n/ obtained. The author speculates that one possible reason for errors involving [d̶] and [z] was that the teachers considered these allophones mere variants of a norm, and infrequent at that. However, he inexplicably ignores the obvious interference from English. In place of isolated word practice, the author rightly calls for more drills for these troublesome allophonic distributions using phrases and breath groups.

5) Spanish /l/, /r/ and /R/. These, states the author, agreeing with previous judgements, are the most obvious offenders, which when rendered with values from English betray an accent at once. During the posttest analysis the American /r/ was found to be the most resistant to correction or improvement. Sacks faults textbooks, which have (or had, before 1960) consistently failed to provide adequate descriptions for Spanish /l/. Inability of the participants to produce Spanish /r/ is seen as more the responsibility of the teacher, rather than inadequate textbook descriptions. Nor does Sacks fail to mention that /r/ can be downright difficult, regardless of explanation and "helpful hints." The author does not venture to cite examples of the various techniques (other than to discredit a common one) employed to solve the problem, and he does not leave the impression that several or a combination of approaches were used to aid the /r/-troubled participants. [See No. 36 for aids in teaching /r/ and /r̄/.]

6) Stress problems with final *-ia, -ía, -io, -ío,* and *-ió.* Speculation on the possible interfering stress patterns.

7) Problems of three-syllable stress patterns. The teachers were particularly guilty of misplaced stresses on the penult syllable. Questions cognates being a distinct advantage in learning, since they account for many stresses and other mistakes in phonology.

8) Errors caused by a dominant (majority) pattern. *Veinte* > *viente,* since *ie* abounds in Spanish, but *ei* does not. Also, errors in stress involving final *-n* and *-s.*

9) Pronunciation errors due to the influence of spelling. Most of the familiar instances in Spanish when, atypically, there is a lack of one-to-one correspondence between graph and sound (phoneme). Or when the student encounters negative transfer from English (e.g., *qu, gu, z,* etc.).

Sacks' conclusions: 1) Errors in pronunciation generally fall into patterns (and thus can be readily analyzed), and appropriate drills can be devised to correct the mistakes; 2) The obvious solution to bad pronunciation habits is not to form them in the first place. Most remedial work of this kind would not be needed if proper attention were given to phonology in the very first days of FL instruction; 3) Attention should be given to the articulatory nature of the sounds being learned (along with the contrastive similarities and differences of English); and 4) The conventional phonetics courses should become courses in phonetics and phonemics (phonology), which would include description and drill. (This has already been accomplished in many FL programs around the country.)

Not surprisingly, the teacher participants whose Spanish is described in this study committed the same kinds of pronunciation errors common to the average group of English-speaking learners.

[For a fuller analysis, especially for cognate patterns, see Nos. 28 and 35.]

34. SACKS, NORMAN P.
"Peninsular and American Spanish," in *A Handbook for Teachers of Spanish and Portuguese*, edited by Donald D. Walsh. Lexington, Mass.: D. C. Heath and Co., 1969, 36-42.

A discussion of pedagogical dualism concerning the decision as to whether to choose Peninsular or American Spanish. Though this article is concerned with both cultural and linguistic aspects of the question, focus is on phonological differences. The author points out that too many teachers oversimplify the phonetic and phonemic variations found within the different dialectal areas. Examples of this tendency are given, along with the significant characteristics common to but absent from supposedly authentic varieties used in the classroom.

A consideration of the notion of "purity" of pronunciation—what criteria to follow in choosing a particular dialect for students.

The author suggests that the great majority of teachers in reality teach a Hispanic pronunciation that is a blend of many phonologic features not all common to any one dialect. [For a further discussion of this question, see Nos. 5 and 23.]

35. STOCKWELL, ROBERT P. and J. DONALD BOWEN
The Sounds of English and Spanish. (Contrastive Structure Series.) Chicago and London: The University of Chicago Press, 1965. xi + 168 pp.

A contrastive study of the sound systems of English and Spanish. It has a companion volume on the grammatical systems of these languages [See No. 70]. Both represent to a significant degree pioneering ventures in the field of applied linguistics, for each brings together for the first time rather complete inventories of the teaching problems likely to confront the teacher of Spanish. Some of the information contained in the volume on phonology is to be found in an earlier treatment, a drillbook, by the same authors [See No. 19].

Contents: 1) The structure of sound systems; 2) Sound systems in conflict; 3) Stress, rhythm, and intonation patterns; 4) The articulation of consonants and vowels; 5) The consonant systems of Spanish and English; 6) The consonant sequences of English and Spanish; 7) The vowel systems; 8) Summary of segmental elements; 9) Appendix: the teaching of pronunciation; 10) Glossary of terms; 11) Abbreviations and symbols; 12) Supplement on distinctive-feature systems of English and Spanish sounds.

The first chapter accomplishes a clear presentation of linguistic principles as applied to identifying and analyzing phonologic interference between target and native languages. Chapter 2 establishes a very useful hierarchy of these phonological problems according to degree of difficulty, functional load, potential mishearing and pattern congruity. Strong features of the chapters treating the consonants and vowels: isolation of student errors and good examples (with explanations) of these typical errors.

Though the authors advocate no particular teaching method, they lean toward audiolingual procedures stressing practice of oral habits before introducing written work. In the Appendix on the teaching of pronunciation the teacher is urged to provide his students with guidance as to where, how, and why pronunciation problems will occur. The authors do not hesitate to suggest that when all else fails the teacher should resort to detailed explanation of the troublesome areas.

Advanced students, in particular graduate students, will want to go beyond an understanding of the articulation and distribution of allophones and phonemes and can study with profit the distinctive feature analysis of Spanish and English sounds in the Supplement (prepared by John W. Martin).

This text has been widely used in classes in Spanish phonetics and phonemics.

[Reviewed by Ann Tukey, *LL*, 17 (July, 1967), 71-74.]

36. WRIGHT, LEAVITT O.
    "Five Spanish *R*'s: How to Approach Them," *Hisp*, 45
    (December, 1962), 742-743.

Admitting that some students simply aren't able to reproduce Spanish
/r/ and /r̄/ on first (or even last) try, the author shares some of his
successful techniques. His basic approach is through imitation of English
words containing near equivalents to the tap or multiple trill phonemes.
(For /r/: "A pod o' pease;" when + Consonant: "oddity," pronounced
rapidly). Since /r̄/ can prove to be even more difficult, Wright suggests that
the teacher by-pass it until the student has mastered the single tap or flap
r. The real "trick" is never to give up, to urge the learner to work at the
problem sound. The author suggests some phrases which have produced
good results for him (*"para la parra," "pero el perro,"* etc.).

Not included in these suggestions are the various kinds of descriptive
(articulation) approaches, which can be especially helpful with older
students.

III.   Teaching Grammar

37. BEBERFALL, LESTER

"Spanish Verb Forms by Conversion," *MLJ*, 47 (March, 1963), 103-106.

Advances a procedure for teaching and testing the verb morphology of the five simple tenses of the indicative and the two of the subjunctive in Spanish. The total steps involved in working through these forms require a rewrite format:

preferir	El estudiante diligente . . . no	prefiere[1]
prefiere tú	(hace mucho)	prefería[2]
preferid vosotros	(ayer)	prefirió
‾‾‾‾‾‾‾‾‾‾‾‾‾‾‾	(mañana)	preferirá
no prefieras tú	(Yo dije ayer que mañana)	preferiría
no prefiráis vosotros		
prefiera Ud.	Es posible que el estudiante no	prefiera[1]
no prefiera Ud.	(hace mucho)	prefiriese
no prefieran Uds.		prefiriera
prefiramos nosotros		
no prefiramos nosotros		

The model (practice) sentence incorporated into this scheme is *"El estudiante diligente europeo de inglés no prefiere conversar en su propio idioma con el estudiante americano de lengua extranjera."* The numbers are used to correlate the indicative and subjunctive tenses as to time orientation. The student begins with the simple indicative sentence and, using "leaders" to elicit other verb possibilities, including the subjunctive, progresses through the seven sentences with their different verb inflections. The number and person of the verb can of course be changed to exhaust the paradigm.

The left hand margin, headed here by the infinitive *preferir*, is devoted to listing the commands. The *tú* and *vosotros* commands are separated from the others and their negative forms follow immediately from them to impress on the student the overt but difficult-to-learn differences.

The cues to elicit the different forms are necessary for constructing new sentences, but are no substitute for a meaningful context. One guesses that the procedure given here is the second of a three-step operation, the first being an even more mechanical memorizing of all the verb forms to be used, the third, an exercise to free the practiced forms from their contrived contexts. If not for this last vital step, the student will never proceed beyond the unusable mechanical level of "language" control. Beberfall admits that a student's success with morphology is no greater than "his understanding of how the constructions are used in context." Some teachers will accept the author's building-conversion procedure as preparatory to spontaneous expression.

38. BOLINGER, DWIGHT L.
    "Reference and Inference: Inceptiveness in the Spanish Preterite," *Hisp*, 46 (March, 1963), 128-135.

Studies the commonly ignored "inceptive" aspect often signaled when the preterite verb form is used in Spanish. Even when textbook treatments do include some inceptive usages, Bolinger correctly points out, they are normally treated merely as translation problems (as with *saber* or *conocer*).

Adopting Bull's terms (cyclic vs. noncyclic) [Taken from *Time, Tense and the Verb* — see Appendix] to describe the initiative/terminative aspects of events represented by the preterite, the author endeavors to settle the question of whether the feature of inceptiveness is a part of the Spanish verb *system* (*sic*) or, instead, an inherent trait of only certain verbs.

Disagreeing with Bull, Bolinger argues that some cyclic verbs in the preterite are not necessarily terminative (*"El médico me examinó a la una"*). Avoiding context words that impose one aspect or the other, the author next questions that noncyclic events are initiative. Although Bolinger's reasoning is more or less cogent, some of his examples are not entirely convincing. He does manage, however, to come up with a few examples of preterites which seem not to be tied to either the initiative or the terminative aspect.

The author maintains that the nature of the event contributes to its inceptiveness or terminativeness, regardless of the cyclic or noncyclic distinction. Citing those verbs which in their preterite forms ordinarily signal initiation (*saber, conocer*, etc.), Bolinger views them as holding both acquisitive and retentive phases (or meanings) and the preterite morpheme simply selects the most appropriate meaning, the one that "fits." *Saber, conocer* and other verbs belong, because of their equivocal potentials, to a superclass. The author adds to his list of the *saber-conocer* type, verbs such as *decir, afirmar*, and the verbs of perception (*ver, notar*, etc.) as well. These and others exhibit the same kind of duality and can be both cyclic or noncyclic. This analysis is more complex than Bull's and also more difficult to test.

In calling into question the claim that the preterite in Spanish contains an initiative aspect, Bolinger points out these basic misconceptions: 1) The correlation between inceptiveness or terminativeness and cyclic vs. noncyclic events; 2) No distinction between reference and inference; 3) The ignoring of multiple labeling for a berb; and 4) The requirement that the preterite explicitly label the beginning, middle or end of an event.

Bolinger maintains that the reference of the preterite is a constant and when it appears to vary the context accounts for this variation, and that the preterite refers to a segment of anteriority. When we use the preterite we may be more interested in one end of the segment than in the other, but this is determined by the nature of the verb and by its specific context.

If Bolinger's conclusions are correct, they have important implications for the teacher, for decisions regarding grammar (drill) material and its presentation rest on the accepted analysis of this problem involving a high-frequency component of the complex Spanish verb system.

39. BOLINGER, DWIGHT L.
"Three Analogies," *Hisp*, 44 (March, 1961), 134-137.

Bolinger emphasizes the importance, in teaching both the FL lexicon and its grammar, of being able to establish and use statements (including translations and paraphrases) of equivalency between the two languages. If, for example, the teacher cannot easily demonstrate some idea or event (entities are easier to get across), then perhaps his best or at least most economical solution is to come out and explain the exact meaning of the FL segment. The greater the abstract quality of the information, and the more the two languages diverge in verbalizing reality organized in different ways, the less likely one is to find neat equivalences. Therefore, translation must be substituted for demonstration.

The author offers three instances for consideration, one involving a transformation and two, the prosodic features of length and pitch.

1) No single stratagem or any combination of them has been found to solve the various inevitable problems with Spanish *gustar*. That is, no way has been found to keep the student from inferring incorrect assumptions. Equating *please* with *gustar*, while solving the problem of word order, creates other obstacles. The suggestion is to substitute *appeal* for *like* or *please*, as it takes an indirect object and poses no problems of verbal aspect ("They are pleas*ing* to him").

2) The verb *poder* ordinarily can be used for English *may* + infinitive. However, the corresponding Spanish utterance favors a clause (*He may not come > Puede que no venga*, less commonly, *Puede no venir*). Complicating matters is the use of *may* with another meaning and calling for an infinitive in Spanish: *Puede sentarse.*. Though the obvious way of handling this is to state the difference semantically, there exists a formal difference when English *may* means "possibility," in which case that verb is stressed, but not when stating "permission." The contrast of stress, then, can be used as the controlling cues for the Spanish.

3) Simple declarative statements in Spanish will sound emphatic or contain inappropriate contrast if the student simply transfers the

analogous English pattern. Various kinds of incorrect inferences can be drawn by the hearer when the sentence carries foreign intonation features. Bolinger's general advice is for the nonnative to make his Spanish statements sound like commands in English. There are exceptions to this patterning, however, and the teacher would be well-advised to keep a sharp ear attuned to all the basic sentence intonational patterns he hears during the formative period of FL study.

40. BOWEN, J. DONALD and TERENCE MOORE
"The Reflexive in English and Spanish: A Transformational Approach," *TESOLQ*, 2 (March, 1968), 12-26.

Introduces the topic with a discussion of linguistic universals, linguistic competence, and linguistic performance. Next, the morphology, function and constraints of the reflexive systems of English and Spanish are discussed. The Spanish set of forms is cited for its smaller inventory and atypical, reduced concordance. (In Spanish the only identity that need be established in the third person is with the subject; English indicates gender and number: *se lastimó* vs. *He (she) hurt himself (herself)*, etc.) But Spanish matches English in most reflexive rules: Reflexivization occurs when two referentially identical noun phrases are contained within the same sentence; neither language allows a reflexive to refer to a preceding noun that is not the subject of the sentence; both languages have certain verbs with which reflexive pronouns are obligatory.

But Spanish has more verbs which must appear with reflexive pronouns. And English usage permits certain ambiguities ("He kept the candy near him") which do not occur in the Spanish equivalents. In general, the reflexive device has more applications in Spanish than in English. Spanish will make use of it with verbs (*sentarse, alegrarse*) that are normally considered intransitive in English. Spanish also allows the reflexive in the agent deletion pattern. The reflexive for "unplanned occurrences" (*Se me olvidó*) is possible in Spanish because there is no restriction against a reflexive pronoun referring back to an inanimate subject. Still another difference is the use of the reflexive in Spanish with certain verbs to express the idea that an action is carried to its logical and final conclusion (*comerse, irse*, etc.). An English translation is difficult to find for the *se* construction when an extension of agent deletion, with no subject expressed (*Se trabaja mucho aquí*), since omitting a subject is not allowed in English. The authors do not like an explanation which considers *se* the subject of these verbs, because to do so is to assign a unique function to this Spanish reflexive form.

Fourteen transfer problems are described in terms of the student's use and avoidance of the reflexive. These are listed in order of decreasing importance for the learner.

Bowen and Moore correctly rank the reflexive high on the list of learning problems. Though not a detailed study, this account of the forms and functions of the reflexive in Spanish and English is helpful in determining the best teaching strategies, including the matter of sequent order of structures.

41. BULL, WILLIAM E. and ENRIQUE E. LAMADRID
"Our Grammar Rules Are Hurting Us," *MLJ*, 55 (November, 1971), 449-454.

With an unprecedented crisis facing the foreign-language profession, characterized by a questioning of relevance in general and the effectiveness of teaching, along with the consequent demand that the FL requirement either be reduced or completely abolished, the teacher must stop to examine the current status of his subject in the curriculum. For whatever reasons, the new-direction '50's and the bandwagoning '60's failed to develop FL instruction into what the authors refer to as "a marketable product." Bull and Lamadrid suggest that mediocre student achievement can in large part be attributed to the fact that many rules and exercises are either "linguistically inadequate, difficult to decode, sometimes utterly meaningless and, with a surprising frequency, just plain wrong." At least fifty percent of the rules now in use are judged to fall into these categories.

The authors maintain that we now have proof that the FL learner learns faster and better when he is fully conscious of what he is performing and learning. Rules can only be of two varieties: 1) those that tell the student where the native and target languages overlap, with no interference, and 2) those that state accurately how the second language differs from the student's own and provide him with the cues for choice of the appropriate FL behavior. The perfect rule "guides the student to a perfect imitation of the native *in all cases*." Here is the source of much rule information the authors find misleading. For example, the descriptive adjective that "usually" follows the noun it modifies does so only a little more than fifty percent of the time. Another involves the unwanted subject pronoun in Spanish, for which the English speaker cannot ascertain redundancy from the Spanish point of view.

Bull and Lamadrid go on to cite a score of misleading or imperfect rules, involving the imperfect and preterite, gender, mood, the article, various verb functions, etc. Included in the discussion are non-rules ("The imperfect indicative is used to express statements about location") and "all except" rules ("When referring to clothing or parts of the body, the definite article is used instead of the possessive adjective, except when the possessive is needed for clarification"). Since "all except" rules in fact consist of two (or more) parts, the authors suggest that they be rewritten as two rules.

No textbooks were found to be free from the biggest offender: rules that are patently wrong. The authors are at a loss to explain why so many bad rules have continued to be forced upon the unknowing student. The only explanation would be that the profession is victim to its own traditions, which have stressed the importance of literature rather than applied linguistics. Classical tradition and its improper application is also blamed.

Bull and Lamadrid are discouraged, and rightly so, that the available correct rules have not found their way into the latest materials. They maintain a radical view; namely, that the FL teaching profession has isolated itself from the mainstream of linguistic research, "instinctively seeking security in a return to the traditional grammar of a generation ago." Elsewhere in the literature, one hears from the group representing the other extreme, which is convinced that current methods or approaches are too "linguistic," with not enough emphasis on technique and the total learning environment.

Even granting support to some middle stand, no one can find fault with the authors' concern for better rules. While some of the rules cited in this study are so obviously poor that they surely belong to texts (unidentified) not widely used, this does not excuse them. And all producers of materials should keep before them a vision of the growing numbers of FL teachers who will no longer be satisfied with imperfect hand-me-down grammar rules.

42. CARFORA, JUANITA
> "*Lo* and *Le* in American Spanish," *Hisp*, 51 (May, 1968), 300-302.

Carfora does not like the cursory treatment given the troublesome verb pronouns *lo* and *le* in textbooks. She especially doesn't like the omission of *le* from the list of direct object pronouns, or grammars that give *lo* as the usual form in Spanish America with the suggestion that the student use *lo* for a direct object, *le* for an indirect object.

The pronunciamentos of the *Real Academia* and the findings of Bello, Ramsey, Kany, Keniston and others are cited. Not surprisingly, their statements do not represent a consensus.

Since the author saw no attempt on the part of these grammarians to identify an underlying explanation for the inconsistency in the usage, she worked up a questionnaire in 1965 which was distributed to ninety-four Latin American informants. Sixty sentences from random texts and with *lo* and *le* in all syntactic distributions were used. Results of the tabulation: 1) 3339 appearances of *lo*, 2019 of *le*; 2) Very few respondents allowed free variation of the pronouns; 3) *Le* is commonly used as a direct object for persons, either in conversation or in writing; 4) *Le* is seen to replace *lo* in sentences with *a usted* and with references to persons of high social rank (i.e., to show respect); 5) A decided preference for *le* with the verb *creer* (so as not to change its meaning), more consistently with *pagar* and *ganar*; 6) No consistent usage when two object pronouns occurred.

Neither sentence structure, verb form, nor age, sex, etc. of the informant governed the choice of pronouns. The only determining factors appeared to be etiquette and personal relationship.

Different kinds of questionnaire formats, stressing structure and content factors, would doubtless reveal additional distinctions.

43. CRESSEY, WILLIAM W.
"Teaching Irregular Present Tense Verb Forms: A Transformational Approach," *Hisp*, 55 (March, 1972), 98-100.

Proposes the application of rules in transformational phonology to the teaching of certain Spanish irregular verbs. Though not stressing the point, Cressey would limit this strategy to present tense forms, and only some of these. He correctly demonstrates that while forms such as the one-syllable *doy, soy,* [*e*]*stoy* lend themselves pedagogically to transformational formulations, others do not; namely, those irregularities which if given in appropriate citation forms would obscure vital information.

Not new, but certainly deserving further deliberation is the suggestion that instead of teaching stem *o > ué, e > ié*, a conjugated form, specifically third person singular, replace the infinitive as the first introduction to a Spanish verb. Thus: *cuenta > contar,* a reversal. For *-ar* verbs there is no problem, since the new citation form would preserve the conjugation distinction; but *-er* vs. *-ir* (*puede, miente*) would coalesce as to infinitive class. It is questionable that the student gains more in noting radical vowel behavior than he loses in ignoring the conjugation distinctions. The real question is whether or not students can be expected to learn simultaneously the root vowel information and the conjugation identity, perhaps with equal competence.

Cressey wonders when teachers might expect dictionaries and textbooks to contain this new approach to the troublesome irregular verbs.

In general audiolingual teaching facilitates this approach and the convinced instructor can generally use and stress the third person singular forms.

44. CRESSEY, WILLIAM W.
"Teaching the Position of Spanish Adjectives: A Transformational Approach," *Hisp*, 55 (December, 1969), 878-881.

Since the position of the descriptive adjective is constant in English, but not in Spanish, students of Spanish often experience difficulties in determining correct placement of these adjectives in noun phrases. The author believes this problem can be lessened by taking advantage of the available positive transfer from related structures which exist in both native and target languages. Those who deny the value of positive transfer from one language to the other may accept Cressey's position, however, for his pedagogical proposal is built primarily on similarities within the target language.

Before demonstrating the possibilities for teaching position of the descriptive adjective, the author reviews the published attempts to correct faulty rules governing the Spanish adjective in noun clauses. Although textbooks written since the righting of the old rules have generally incorporated the clarifications, and even rely on positive transfer, Cressey points out that they have not made use of related structures in the case of the adjective in nominal constructions.

The transformational analysis here of noun phrases such as *los hombres valientes* and *los valientes araucanos* is that they are actually derived from relative clause constructions containing the verb *to be.* Thus: *los hombres que son valientes > los hombres valientes*; *los araucanos, que son valientes, ... > los valientes araucanos.* The rules that involve the concept of restrictivity are born out in punctuation; the commas that set off the clause in the second example indicate that the clause is non-restrictive. The author posits two important pedagogical inferences, once the correspondence between the restrictive and the non-restrictive clause has been established: 1) The student can take advantage of the already familiar concept of restriction, and 2) Useful pattern drills can be built on the analytic devices provided by transformational grammar. Sample pattern drill possibilities are outlined; the student first practices cases of restriction, then non-restriction, and finally a mixture of the two.

This excellent article should suggest other possibilities for the application of TG devices in teaching FL structures.

45. DALBOR, JOHN B.

"A Simplified Tagmemic Approach for Teaching Spanish Syntax," *Hisp*, 55 (September, 1972), 490-497.

Outlines a simplified tagmemic, or slot-and-filler, approach for teaching Spanish syntax in an elementary college course sequence. Only an abbreviated version of the entire system, made up of both phrase-structure and transformational components, is presented. An important feature of the method is that it emphasizes functions of the conceptualized components (actor, complement, adverbial of place, etc.).

The basic syntactic unit is the clause, developed as to tagmemic slots and its deep to surface structure levels. Clause patterns are determined by the occurrence of certain obligatory tagmemes with specified functions. The top level is the broad syntactical or relational level; the second is the function level; the third, the morphological level; and lastly, the "manifest" level (represented orthographically):

	S	P
1.		
2.	actor	NDV*
3.	noun	verb
4.	Juan	trabaja

*Non-directive verb, i.e., does not take a DO or IO complement.

Dalbor uses three basic clause patterns, each with optional (adverbial, prepositional) slots. Essentially they are predicated on the verbs they contain: intransitive (NDV), transitive (direct object, indirect object), and linking. A verb like *hablar* functions as both a directive and a non-directive.

Transformational modifications are sketched, with each level shown. Complications involving "nesting" and "branching" are avoided and in general simplicity of presentation is achieved for pedagogical purposes. Dalbor quite cleverly negotiates some of the would-be unruly situations as regards format.

The author proposes that all the basic and most of the sub-patterns be taught and drilled before the modifications are introduced. He contends that the majority of major problem areas of Spanish syntax can be handled with this approach.

Importantly this strategy brings into clear focus the need to pay more attention to sequent presentation of syntactic components in their most appropriate hierarchical order.

Dalbor is correct in insisting that students need an approach that deals with the syntactic components of the FL as related and organized elements, and perhaps his plan succeeds more than others in this respect. Reliance on the visual aspect of language will please some teachers. The question is, of course, whether or not most or even all students benefit more from this kind of deliberate cognitive mental activity than from a greater amount of practice, assuming oral goals; for, after all, only so much time is available for any combination of study and practice. Actually, Dalbor's suggestion is not that his presentation of the grammar replace the usual kinds of audiolingual practice, but instead that it precede drilling and translation. He strongly holds that the understanding his strategy affords will render the learner more willing to perform the less appealing exercises.

46. DALBOR, JOHN B.
    "Temporal Distinctions in the Spanish Subjunctive," *Hisp*, 52 (December, 1969), 889-896.

Investigates the use of the subjunctive in subordinate noun and adjective clauses in Spanish. In order to verify the "elusive aspects" of the Spanish subjunctive in relation to sequence of tenses, a questionnaire was designed to gather the necessary data—information not found by the author in prior studies on this topic. Conventional use of the term "tense" is applied in discussing the temporal distinctions made by native speakers. In the main Dalbor operates within the framework of the Spanish verb system as established in the more recent literature [See especially No. 5], and his thinking and presentation are clear. One potential confusion for the reader, however, is the introductory observation regarding the consequences of a reduced set of subjunctive tenses, producing the loss of certain temporal distinctions contained by the indicative set. These are more likely distinctions of aspect and order, not of time.

    The principal focus of this study, and the questionnaire items from which it is made, is the question of how the Spanish speaker renders a past event in the subjunctive after a present verb in the main clause. But other combinations were included in the questionnaire, whose format consisted of an indicative sentence on the left and, to the right, a corresponding cue to elicit the preferred subjunctive version (*Creo que llegó* (or *llegaba*): *No creo que* ___.). All sentences were checked by educated speakers for authenticity. The respondents were fifty native speakers representing a wide dialectal range.

    Though certainly not as reliable as spontaneous speech, the questionnaires revealed these patterns:

    1) Forty-nine percent of the natives wrote in the present perfect subjunctive for a completed past action after a main verb in the present (*Creo que vieron la película* > *Espero que hayan visto la película*). Thirty

percent favored the past subjunctive (*vieran, viesen*). Relative recency of the prior action did not seem to determine the choice. Dalbor suggests a possible fuzziness in the native's concept or perception of remoteness. Most probably the determinant is the specific time orientation of the dependent verb.

2) Bearing out the usual statement in grammars, almost 80 percent of the respondents gave the present subjunctive form for posterior-to-present (i.e., future) action (*escribirá > escriba*).

3) Unexpectedly, the present subjunctive rather than the past subjunctive was the preference for the conditional (for a hypothetical event) in adjective clauses after a main present verb (*Tengo uno que serviría > Busco uno que sirva*).

4) When the subordinate action was anterior to a past verb, the past perfect subjunctive was the preferred from (*Creía que ya habían cerrado las ventanas > No creía que ya cerraran . . .*).

5) For sentences with the main verb in the past and subordinate verb in the preterite: (*Encontró a un estudiante que vio el accidente > No encontró a nadie que viera* [54 percent]; . . . *que hubiera visto* [19 percent]).

6) The past subjunctive was used in more than 70 percent of the responses to replace the posterior-to-past (i.e., the conditional) form (*perdería > perdiera*).

7) Choice of the past subjunctive for a simultaneous past (imperfect) event prior to either a past or present main verb.

Dalbor proposes that these majority usages be taught to students rather than confusing them with free variation, and that these sequences of tenses can perhaps best be taught via transformational techniques instead of recourse to "meaning."
[See No. 49 for another analysis of this problem.]

47. DINNES, IRIS SINDING
    "Must All Unclassified Spanish Words Be Memorized for Gender?", *Hisp*, 54 (September, 1971), 487-492.

Suggests the possibility of predicting the gender of those Spanish nouns which have neither inherent gender nor the characteristic word-final gender-bearing sounds or letters. In other words, that group of nouns whose gender must be memorized individually. It might be the case that native speakers of Spanish are at least partially aware of certain gender-sound relationships not described in current grammatical descriptions and teaching materials.

Based on a limited, though random word sample, the author concludes that there appears to be a correspondence between "gender" (Meaning an -*o* vs. an -*a* noun) and phonological patterning. Dinnes' findings are as follows:

1. Nouns probably masculine:
   1) uncommon words with a stressed /a/ in the first syllable;
   2) words with diphthongs (especially /ai/ and /au/ in the stressed syllable;
   3) words of one syllable except those ending in *z*;
   4) words ending in a stressed syllable, except with final /r, l, *ón*);
   5) polysyllabic words (the more syllables, the higher the probability).
2. Nouns probably feminine:
   1) common words with a stressed /a/ in the first syllable;
   2) most words with a stressed /ie/ (and, fewer, with /ue/);
   3) words ending in *z*;
   4) scientific words with final /is/.

These "rules" are subject to more exhaustive sampling. Should these patterns, or some of them, plus others, prove dependable, then the student's job of gender memorization will be lessened. It would be premature, however, to accept the limited evidence set forth in this article as sufficient for the problem. The great majority of the words cited are masculine, which suggests the possibility than in general the so-called unclassifiable nouns are masculine. This being the case, it is not difficult to seek and find certain phonological pattern groups. Further investigation would clarify the matter.

48. DOUGLASS, R. THOMAS
   "Gerundive and Non-Gerundive Forms," *Hisp*, 50 (March, 1967), 99-103.

Restates but for the most part gives Bull's [See No. 5] presentation of verbal aspect, focusing on the /-*do*/ and /-*ndo*/ signals. Douglass pulls together the very incisive and useful information on the Spanish verb system found in several chapters of the comprehensive study by Bull. He begins with an explanation of the possible aspectual relationships that exist between an event and the time axis to which it belongs. He then goes into the question of how Spanish uses /-*do*/ and /-*ndo*/ to mark these (five) distinctions.

Several important weaknesses mar Douglass' analysis. One is his view of the future perfective, or "futuritive," as he chooses to label it—to no obvious advantage over any others. Another flaw is his oversimplification of the real meaning of /-*ndo*/, which he sees simply as "imperfective," and redundant with /-*ába*~-*ía*/ in, for example, *estaba cantando.* By not accepting a separate aspectual function for /-*ndo*/, its function is reduced to "emphasis on the imperative idea." No mention is made of an "action in progress" possibility.

The few references, with examples, of the initiative/perfective aspects are dubious, if not altogether incorrect, although in general the author is rather successful in demonstrating correspondences between a particular verb (cyclic vs. nóncyclic), its morphological possibilities and the speaker's communication desires. Conclusions: The usually redundant gerundive form is normally identical in aspect to the corresponding non-gerundive form and regularly signals emphasis or restriction.

49. FARLEY, RODGER A.
"Sequence of Tenses: A Useful Principle?", *Hisp*, 48 (September, 1965), 549-553.

Questions the validity of patterns of sequence of tenses in Spanish and their presentation in teaching. The principle or rule Farley is referring to states that the time of a dependent verb in the subjunctive is determined by the tense of another verb, usually that of the independent clause which precedes it. In studying this question, the author notes that textbook writers have acknowledged that this rule does not hold up and have felt the need to liberally qualify their statements with such terms as "generally," "normally," "provided," and so on.

Exceptions to this basic principle, and the ones which Farley examines, involve sequences in which 1) a past subjunctive follows a present tense verb, and 2) a present subjunctive follows a past tense verb. Based on the rules found in some widely used textbooks, the author concludes that students will be misled into believing that only certain or all combinations of tenses are possible, or that good grammar insists that the verbs in both clauses must be marked by the same time. ("Tense" is used in this article to mean "conjugation," rather than simply time.)

Farley finds eleven patterns of usage in everyday Spanish which run contrary to the familiar rules. His examples are taken from newspapers, plays and native conversation.

These are the author's exception patterns:
1) Present + Imperfect Subjunctive (where the dependent verb signals a past event or a conditional present or future one)
2) Present + Pluperfect Subjunctive (with the subjunctive used as a "migratory form to express a hypothesis pertaining to past time")
3) Command + Present Perfect Subjunctive

4) Command + Imperfect Subjunctive (for past or contrary-to-fact idea)
5) Command + Pluperfect Subjunctive
6) Present Perfect + Perfect Subjunctive
7) Present Perfect + Imperfect Subjunctive (to express anteriority to the present moment and posteriority to both present and past axis of reference)
8) Imperfect + Present Subjunctive
9) Preterite + Present Subjunctive (signaling future, or posterior action)
10) Conditional + Present Subjunctive
11) Imperfect Subjunctive + Present Subjunctive ("a future from a past future," actually a simple future subjunctive, to establish posterior order without another present verb to establish the time)

It would be difficult, if not impossible, to ascertain all the verbal aspects for especially the last two patterns without reference to context. Order and time are the principle variables and, as Farley points out, "the educated Spanish-speaking native uses as many combinations ... as the sense of his communication calls for." And this does not contradict the frequent patterns of Present + Present and Past + Past. But, as is correctly demonstrated, recourse to out-of-context English sentences for comparison and translation and blind application of the rule based on relative frequency are not desirable. Even if one suspects that native speakers would reject some of Farley's example sentences, most of them substantiate his thesis; namely, that the student needs better information than either the pat rule or unclear or incomplete descriptions of the occurring combinations. This information, we should stress, includes a thorough understanding of the complex Spanish verb system.

50. FARLEY, RODGER A.
"Time and the Subjunctive in Contemporary Spanish," *Hisp*, 53 (September, 1970), 466-475.

The author's second investigation [See No. 49] of the use of the subjunctive in Spanish. As in the first, Farley seeks out the patterns and adds nine new sequences to his original eleven. Some of these would not have a high frequency of occurrence and some contain ellipsis, which explains the infrequent combinations, but the more than two thousand examples of the subjunctive taken from fifteen modern Spanish plays corroborate the main thesis; namely, that a sequence of indicative and subjunctive forms within an independent/dependent syntactic framework is as common or rare as the necessity to express the thought requiring the combination and that the time signaled in the subjunctive verb conforms to the logic of the discourse. Ninety percent of the verbs tabulated are simple forms and the ratio of present to past is approximately three to one.

After Farley reviews the subjunctive tenses as established in his data he suggests the following pedagogical approach:

1) Impress on the students that no one-to-one correspondence exists between Spanish and English forms.

2) Make certain that the learner always relates the time of the event to the tense (form). This understanding can easily be lost in certain types of pattern drilling.

3) Drills should be used to illustrate the multi-time potentials of the subjunctive forms. This can be accomplished in conjunction with charts (as described here) representing both time axes in their "extended time" dimensions.

Some readers will be confused by the author's designations for order sequence, in particular his Pre Post-Past, Post Pre-Present, Post Pre-Past, etc. labels. Less complicated descriptions are available which account for the same information.

[See Nos. 5 and 46.]

51. FELDMAN, DAVID M.
   "A Syntactic Verb-Unit in Spanish," *Hisp*, 45 (March, 1962), 86-89.

Using constituent analysis, the author discusses the auxiliary + infinitive construction in Spanish, with these four possibilities: 1) different subjects for the auxiliary and the infinitive, which functions as objective complement (*le oí hablar*); 2) the auxiliary and the infinitive are separated by a morpheme, usually a relator word (*voy a hacerlo*); 3) the infinitive is the subject of the auxiliary (*me gusta cantar*); 4) the auxiliary and the infinitive share the same subject but are not separated by anything. The author studies in particular the last of these constructions.

Feldman finds earlier attempts to describe this verbal construct faulty in that neither semantic nor normative grammatical statements have provided adequate descriptions. In attempting to attribute to the "verbal paraphrase" in Spanish distinctions of "mood" signaled by inflection in the parent language, it appears that Feldman has confused some of the verbal signals sent by modern Spanish, or at least the reader can be confused by a lack of clear definition of or distinction between "mood verbs" and "modal verbs." Complicating matters is the complex nature of the various aspectual distinctions of the verb.

Feldman criticizes the familiar analysis of the auxiliary + infinitive phrase, with the infinitive as direct object of the auxiliary verb. He further questions the accuracy of arriving at this conclusion based on the assumption that auxiliaries such as *querer*, for example, are transitive. In fact, Feldman is unwilling to allow that transitivity can be determined by the syntactic properties of a given lexical (verb) item or its "occurrence" (meaning function—"a verb is neither transitive nor intransitive").

Even more questionable is the author's insistence that *voy a hacerlo* and *quiero hacerlo* represent two different constituent classes, since only for the latter "is it feasible to put the finite verb and the infinitive in the same box" (Feldman represents the underlying structure of his four sentence types in frames within boxes). Because he denies the transitive/intransitive distinction as a valid criterion for deciding segment uniqueness, it is difficult to accept Feldman's separation of the two simply because the relator *a* follows conjugated *ir* before the infinitive. The author's immediate constituent analysis of *Yo quiero comer las manzanas* (*Yo, -o / quier-, comer, manzanas*) is certainly arguable and his reasoning less than convincing. The same can be said for the examples he uses to demonstrate the fallacy in the direct-object analysis and the supposed parallel usages he finds in the Spanish of the *Cid*.

The principal points brought out in this article are important and warrant closer study, for an understanding of the facts will be of direct application in the pedagogical grammar.

52. FISH, GORDON T.
 "Adjectives Fore and Aft: Position and Function in Spanish," *Hisp*, 44 (December, 1961), 700-708.

Dismayed by the absence in many Spanish textbooks of adequate descriptions of position and function of adjectives, and wanting to clarify some erroneous information in Ramsey [See Appendix], Fish endeavors here to isolate the patterns. The author's approach is based on the premise that "Spanish syntax is rigid and logical," that free variation is rare, and that meaning, function and history determine the controlling factors. Unfortunately, modern prose rather than everyday speech serves as corpus for the investigation and, thus, the findings are somewhat reduced in pedagogical usefulness.

Although Fish does not formally define the adjective, he states that "true adjectives" are normally descriptive and that the "normal position" for this class of words is before the noun. Descriptive adjectives, we are told, follow the noun only when selective, and not always then. Quantitative, ordinal, indefinite, demonstrative and possessive adjectives do not name attributes carried by descriptive adjectives. And certain adjectives have rules of their own, applicable in special constructions. When an adjective loses or acquires descriptive value it will change its position and seemingly deviate from the basic syntactic rules.

The Spanish adjectives are classified as either descriptive (selective and nonselective) and nondescriptive. When selective, descriptive adjectives are "precise, factual, outstanding, and expressive of choice of either noun or attribute," as opposed to "vague, affective . . . and do not signal choice," when nonselective. But since maintenance of this dichotomy is not always easy to recognize, the author proceeds to investigate the distributions.

The selective descriptive adjectives include those that are restrictive (*el gato doméstico*), pictorial (*la calle miserable*), and explanatory (*su Mallorca natal*). Exact differences between these categories are perhaps more real than apparent, as Fish, or rather his examples, suggest. The author comments on the futile and unnecessary attempts made in earlier studies of the Spanish adjective to consider all adjectives restrictive. Admitting the possibility of nonrestrictive usage would explain many troublesome counter-cases.

Nonselective adjectives are characterized as frequently of "orbital meaning . . . vague, hard to define, and with many synonyms." Further, they must be in harmony with their noun as determined by the context. Types of adjectives treated in this category: affective (emotion, attitude, etc.), expressing moral or esthetic qualities, out of the ordinary quality (impression), magnitude or extent, universal or inherent quality, etc.

The nondescriptive adjectives are classified as true adjectives, numerals and pronominals, cardinals and ordinals, and indefinites. All normally precede the noun they modify, though contrast is possible for some.

Fish should have given clearer and more complete rules for adjective position, especially when two or more adjectives co-occur.

53. FISH, GORDON T.
"*Lo puede hacer* vs. *puede hacerlo*," *Hisp*, 44 (March, 1961), 137-139.

The author, finding no published solution to the linguistic possibilities expressed in the title, sets out to prove that, based on "Spanish syntax . . . ever subject to Law," the accepted free variation is more apparent than real. His findings are taken from some 300 (mostly literary) examples in which the with-verb pronoun is alternately pre- and post-posed with the infinitive following an auxiliary verb.

Since Fish finds *puede hacerlo* to be the more frequent of the two patterns, he takes it as the norm and treats only *lo puede hacer* in detail.

The two patterns are neither equivalent nor optional, he states, and each is required in certain specifiable situations defined by syntactic and contextual factors.

Usages that require *lo puede hacer* pattern:

1) *Se* = "one," and not the object of the infinitive or participle (*se debe exigir*).

2) *Se* = "one," and used with another with-verb pronoun (*le, les, la,* etc.).

3) With *todo*, which "attracts" the pronoun (*todo lo quiere saber*).

4) When the verb "expresses an action that *directly* affects a *predetermined* direct or indirect object; that is, tells what is done to him . . . [or] for him." Fish found that certain verbs ("writing," "telling," "seeing," "following," "believing," etc.) do not fall into this category of direct influence and therefore the with-verb pronoun follows the infinitive rather than precedes the auxiliary.

5) The central information is carried by the auxiliary (*le creía ver*—in which conjugated *creer* allows the following infinitive and is the essential verb as far as meaning is concerned).

6) Finally, with *ir* and *estar* + *-ndo* (*se fue devolviendo; se estaba incriminando*).

[For a reaction to this article, see J. Cary Davis, "Más sobre *Puede Hacerlo, Lo Puede Hacer*" in *Hisp*, 44 (December, 1961), 708-710. Davis insists that Fish has overlooked the most important determiner for this syntactic variation; namely, rhythmic stress.]

54. FISH, GORDON T.
      "*Se*," *Hisp*, 49 (December, 1966), 831-833.

A note to define and account for the uses of the Spanish pronoun *se* in a more precise way than the usual descriptions found in either pedagogical or linguistic grammars.

Fish enumerates some eleven regular and special functions of the form and traces its status from a personal pronoun "to that of a mere particle, a morpheme, an empty word, a tool, back almost to where it started. . . ."

Classifications: I. **Tripersonal.** 1) reflexive; 2) reflexive with special meanings; 3) with verbs that take a dative of interest, and whose reflexive value is lost in translation (*acabarse, irse*, etc.); 4) "a person or animal acts upon himself," where the English would instead use intransitive verbs or a passive form; 5) action affecting a person (oneself), but brought about by "physical or psychic forces," and the subject is not obviously the agent (*ahogarse, enojarse*, etc.); and 6) actions ordinarily performed on oneself treated as reflexive when performed by another. II. **Unipersonal.** 7) stylistic personification (*Los árboles se inclinaron...*); 8) inanimate entities interact, especially in formal written style; 9) the subject-object relationship is reversed, *se* loses its meaning, in particular with verbs of motion, position, condition; 10) many verbs admit a "personal dative in addition to the *se*," to express accidental and involuntary (lack of responsibility) action; and 11) substitute for the passive (*Se les ve*).

Though Fish has mixed meaning and function in establishing his categories (rather than simply classifying the several uses of *se* formally—See Nos. 5, 40, and 60), he does present the basic information. A fuller analysis requires more attention to the grammatical and conceptual subject-object relations, as well as the kinds of verbs involved.

55. FISH, GORDON T.
"Syntactic Equations," *Hisp*, 45 (December, 1962), 743-744.

Lists some typical and other less common constructions containing *ser* which even advanced students of Spanish don't always know. Mistakes involving this usage can be attributed, according to the author, to the learner's failure to understand that *ser* is a sign of equality in clauses of identification, when the subject and complement are, if not equivalent, at least similar in identity.

Fish establishes three categories for these constructions:

1) Normal identifications, which equate subject and object (or predicate noun). Obvious interference from English "it": "it is he;" "he is the one;" etc.

2) Adverbial identifications, which require an adverb or prepositional phrase in both members of the equation: *En tales momentos era cuando* ... Also: *Allí era* (*el lugar*) *donde* ...

3) Demonstrative adverbs, used with the value of noun or pronoun: *Aquí es la casa Bermúdez. Aquí* = "the place." Similarly, *La escena es en Madrid*, in which *la escena* represents the event, the action ("The action takes place in Madrid.").

In all of these examples *ser* identifies rather than describes and, as the author aptly points out, establishes equivalencies in categories 1) and 2).

56. FISH, GORDON T.
"Two Notes on *Estar*," *Hisp*, 47 (March, 1964), 132-135.

A cautionary note on oversimplification in translating English "be" with a choice between *ser* and *estar*. Arbitrary distinctions between these two Spanish verbs, without attention to etymology or "nuclear meanings" can lead the student away from the real meaning of *estar*, which "still means, however vaguely and figuratively, *stand*...." This being the case, Fish notes, it is difficult to fit the verb into expressions involving movement from one place to another, and often some other verb is required to translate "be."

Examples: *venir/ ¡Qué pintada viene aquella mujer! ; ir/ ¿Cómo iba vestido Luis? ; andar/ ¿Ves que ando cojo?*

On *estar + -ndo* vs. English progressive, Fish judges many textbooks guilty of misleading students through statements about parallel constructions. For example, not only doesn't Spanish use the *-ndo* form to relate momentary or initiative events, but auxiliary *estar*, unlike "empty" English "be," is capable of a whole range of meanings of its own. Also, *estar*, in contrast to its English would-be equivalent, possesses two stresses and Fish attributes the signal of emphasis to this feature. The author fixes its uses to include special interest, insistence (in emotive clauses), or what is uppermost in the mind, unusual or unexpected.

With particular reference to *estar haciendo*, the simple form is used to express regular simultaneous action (*¿Qué haces?*). Nor is the compound form used meaning "to occur" (*¿Qué pasa aquí?*). And *estar* will not always be translated with "to be;" instead, with a verb of continuance ("stay," "remain," "continue," etc.), such as in *No puedes estar existiendo así* ("You can't continue to exist. . .").

57. HOLTON, JAMES S.
"Placement of Object Pronouns," *Hisp*, 43 (December, 1960), 584-585.

Notes that the MLA textbook, *Modern Spanish*, is the first beginning text that does not repeat the traditional description of the ordered occurrence of with-verb pronouns. And that, further, only Spaulding's revision [See Appendix] of Ramsey's grammar presents a correct analysis. *Modern Spanish* treats the data in groups in separate chapters, concluding with the summary arrangement:

		lo
	me	la
se	nos	los
	te	las
		le
		les

Se stands either for reflexive or the allomorph of *le/les.* Thus, the reflexive pronoun precedes all other forms, and rarely do more than two of these appear in combination.

While agreeing that the above information is adequate for a beginning text, Holton points out that it is not entirely accurate. By this the author means that native speakers will generate sequences involving direct object pronouns other than *se* which do precede the indirect forms. Holton also cites examples in violation of the traditional Indirect + Direct Object sequence. To account for these latter cases, and those including *se* as direct object, the author proffers the following chart:

			IO	DO
				le
			le	lo
	te		les	la
se		me		les
	os		(se)	los
				las

Holton's rule reads: "When two or more conjunctive (or with-verb) object pronouns occur with a given verbal phrase, they will appear in the following order of precedence: *se, 2nd person, 1st person, 3rd person.*" The only clarification needed is that for the occurrence of *se* as the first of two third-person pronouns, when the indirect object always precedes the direct object. [See No. 61 for reactions to these suggestions.]

The merit of this presentation is that it accounts for all the possibilities and stresses the patterns, putting particular emphasis on overt differences of person (rather than function). If Holton is correct in saying that pedagogically what the student needs most is an instinctive control of the patterns rather than a total awareness of all the relationships between form and function, then automatic production of the right combinations can be achieved through drilling and some amount of explanation. All teachers will agree that control of two with-verb Spanish pronouns is not all that easy; but since there is a high rate of reoccurrence especially of certain combinations, some of the problems are taken care of with less difficulty than many others for which considerable conflict exists between target and native languages.

58. JACKSON, ROBERT and DWIGHT BOLINGER
    "*Trabajar para,*" *Hisp*, 48 (December, 1965), 884-886.

This interesting note on Spanish *trabajar para* and its similar forms points up two important questions; namely, the difficulty but necessity of relying on native informants for verifying usage, and also the efficacy of resorting to translation as the best means, in this case, of teaching variants of expressions involving the same or similar information.

Variation found in literary citations led the authors to prepare a fill-in-the-blank questionnaire designed to elicit from natives of six countries the equivalents for English "to work for, with, at, in," etc. Since the native speakers did not agree in their responses, few generalizations or specific conclusions were possible.

Though the trustworthiness of the answers taken from the questionnaires appears, at least in some cases, doubtful, the authors do ask themselves the right kinds of questions. And they are fully aware of the difficulties in seeking and obtaining the answers. Some findings: Does *trabajar para* (unlike *trabajar con*, *trabajar en*, etc.) suggest a menial, or truckling status on the part of the worker? This appears often to be the case. On the other hand, the possibility exists that *para* remains neutral, and the actual employee-employer relationship is established, not so much by *para* (or other relator words) as by the verbal and discourse context.

General advice for the teacher: for English "work for" translate *trabajar para*; "work with," *trabajar con*; "work at" or "in," *trabajar en*. *Trabajar por* poses other problems based on the functions of *por*.

59. KIDDLE, LAWRENCE B.
"A Suggestion for Teaching the Spanish *Tuteo*," *LL*, 7:3-4 (1956-57), 25-34.

"The purpose of this study is to summarize and criticize the commonly used approaches to the problem of teaching the Spanish *tuteo* and to offer suggestions for an improved approach." Kiddle surveys the presentation of Spanish *tú* and its aggregate forms in twenty random textbooks and finds the grammatical statements misleading and artificial. Although the *tuteo* forms and usage are generally introduced early in the texts, they are not adequately treated or pursued throughout the materials. In some cases they are downgraded by being enclosed in parentheses or are relegated to footnotes or an appendix. Several authors translate or equate them with *thou* and *ye*, and with no explanation of present-day usage in English.

Kiddle suggests three guiding principles for any textbook presentation of *tuteo:* 1) Early introduction in the text and the class and continued practice, in keeping with true frequency of occurrence; 2) If *thou* and *ye* are given as equivalents of *tú* and *vosotros*, they should be explained as archaic forms and no real translations of the Spanish; and 3) The differences between Spanish American and Peninsular convention should be established. And, importantly, the teacher must do whatever he can to make sure that the student attains a feeling for *tuteo* in all its application.

Basing his information on the reactions of six native speakers from different dialect areas, the author divides his discussion of the *tuteo* into five categories: 1) family relationships; 2) school relationships; 3) superior-inferior relationships; 4) casual relationships; and 5) modification of relationship. No one-to-one relationship is insisted upon without exception. But the facts uphold general patterns of usage, which makes a difficult learning problem a little bit easier than it might be.

When Kiddle tries to establish equations between Spanish and the existing norms for English, especially as regards use of first names in English (which he arbitrarily equates with *tú*), he ignores some polite vs. familiar distinctions. Nonetheless, his advice is sound.

60. LOZANO, ANTHONY G.
"Non-Reflexivity of the Indefinite *Se* in Spanish," *Hisp*, 53 (September, 1970), 452-457.

The argument in this investigation of Spanish *se* is that while the meaning of the passive and the indefinite *se* overlap, they are not identical in either form or meaning. The author finds the presentations of the "reflexive" and "indefinite *se*" in the outstanding textbooks of Spanish to be incomplete and misleading. This is so because none of the analyses considers the crucial lexical features of animate/nonanimate and human/nonhuman. Lozano contends that these distinctions are valid and provide for a system of classification which distinguishes between reflexive forms and the indefinite *se*.

The syntactic consequences of this semantic classification are examined for four sentences: 1) *Se envenenaron los duques* (+ animate, + human); 2) *Se hirieron los toros* (+ animate, - human); 3) *Se vendieron los coches* (- animate, - human); and 4) *Se sepultaron los muertos* (- animate, + human). Demonstrating reflexive vs. reciprocal vs. indefinite *se* functions in derived versions of these sentences, the author points out how disambiguation takes place in the basic sentences, which allow only certain kinds of subject nouns. For example, the readings of reciprocal and reflexive do not obtain for the paraphrases of 3 and 4 above: *Alguien vendió los coches*; *Se sepultó a los muertos* (or *Se sepultaron los muertos*). The -animate feature precludes a reflexive function. Conversely, indefinite *se* is the subject in *Se envenenó a los duques* (1) and *Se hirió a los toros* (2), both requiring the personal *a*. By "subject" Lozano means the "true deep-structure-subject."

As regards a passive construction, neither its surface structure nor its meaning is identical to the indefinite *se* corollary. The author explains the constraints involving agents and uses the patterns of occurrence to corroborate his syntactic categories.

Lozano concludes by stating that any correct description and pedagogical presentation of indefinite *se* must take into account the nature of the subject nouns. Nothing is gained, he proposes, by teaching this *se* as a rewrite of a passive utterance, while *alguien*, for example, can be given as the indefinite subject. The author's caution that the passive entails the unnecessary obstacle of a different word order is not a strong argument against using it as the cue for drilling the indefinite *se*. His purely linguistic reasons are more convincing.

[See two rejoinders: William Moellering, *Hisp*, 54 (May, 1971), 300; and R. N. Sabatini, Hisp, 54 (December, 1971), 883-884.]

61. MOEN, MARY E.
    "The Fable of the Malapropish Affixes," *MLJ*, 50 (January, 1966), 8-11.

Studies the Spanish with-verb pronouns in terms of form, function, and order. Centers discussion around the more traditional presentation (a) of Stockwell, Bowen and Martin [See No. 70] and Holton's (b) earlier table [See No. 57]:

(a)

se	te os	me nos	le lo la les los las

(b)

se	te os	me nos	le les	lo la los las

The author correctly points out that (a) has taken the table of precedence one step further, since *le/les* and *lo/la/los/las* can never co-occur. Samples from both literature and habits of native speakers bear out the fact that this total set never precedes any other with-verb pronoun. Moreover, the author denounces as a false "legend" created by generations of textbook writers the ordering: REFLEX + IO and IO + DO.

Moen is reluctant to allow that these morphemes have independent function, for then the function rules are in conflict with the order rules. On the other hand, to acknowledge independent function, while ignoring the traditional rules, is to generate unacceptable sequences of these pronouns. To solve this dilemma, the author suggests a rewrite rule: *te* + *me* + $_V$1st p. $\rightarrow$ *me* + $_V$1st p. + prepositional phrase (yielding *No me voy de ti*, instead of **No te me voy*.) By utilizing this rule, the misleading descriptions, "direct object" and "indirect object," can be discarded, along with the traditional rule: REFLEX + IO + DO. This new approach avoids any futile attempt to assign three different classifications to one form, such as *me*, which can have but one function. And when there is a choice of morphemes, as for third person, it is based on the nature of the Spanish verb (*ayudarle* but *mirarlo*), and not on any IO vs. DO distinctions Furthermore, no one-to-one correspondences exist for these forms between English and Spanish.

Agreeing with Bull [See No. 5, p. 255], Moen cogently argues for a break with tradition which has emphasized nonexistent form-signal relationships and suggests that Spanish speakers today tend increasingly to disregard some of the distinctions that once obtained.

Instead of the "direct object" – "indirect object" terminology of Latin provenance, which may be unknown to the new student, a new terminology is suggested to handle these eleven pronoun forms—one which would stress and clarify them as personal referents and bound, non-stressed forms.

At any rate, the failure of teachers and textbook writers to break away from this kind of traditional description is seen as having a serious limiting effect on any audiolingual program.

62. MOLINA, HUBERT
> "Transformational Grammar in Teaching Spanish," *Hisp*, 51 (May, 1968), 284-286.

In assessing the possible applications of generative transformational grammar to the teaching of FL, Molina presents the teacher with three alternatives. He can ignore it, try to follow it blindly, or "abstract from it and put some of its principles to the test in the classroom." Only the third decision seems reasonable to the author, who proceeds to try to demonstrate, with Spanish examples, how useful a tool TG can be.

While Molina is not guilty of allowing his open enthusiasm to support the founding of a pedagogical theory based on generative grammar, he overstates current knowledge and understates limitations. He urges the teacher to test out some of the linguistic principles, but provides no guidelines. Nine different question transforms are given for a simple interrogative sentence. The transformational procedures involved would supposedly allow the FL learner to internalize the rules (competence) and thereby control the same information in the same ways as the native speaker. This is less than obvious or demonstrable. Furthermore, we have not discovered the necessary "thoroughly systematized . . . steps."

Many teachers strongly feel, like Molina, that TG holds tremendous promise in FL teaching and that trial-and-error experiences will produce convincing evidence of solid contribution to a better methodology. He is likely right, but we have far to go.

63. MOODY, RAYMOND

"More on Teaching Spanish Adjective Position: Some Theoretical and Practical Considerations," *Hisp*, 54 (May, 1971), 315-321.

A reaction to Cressey's article [See No. 44] which treats the same topic. Moody's conclusion is that the earlier investigation does not suggest an approach which solves the problem of teaching adjective position via transformational procedures. Specifically, Moody challenges the validity of Cressey's assumption that because English and Spanish exhibit parallel concepts and use of restrictivity in adjective clauses, the student is familiar with the basic notion and can readily produce the Spanish equivalents. And even if the English speaker does appreciate the difference between *los araucanos, que son valientes, nunca huyen* (nonrestrictive, with a pause) and this same sentence without a pause (restrictive), Cressey's strategy, which calls for the student to delete and shift in arriving at single adjective usage (*los valientes araucanos* vs. *los araucanos valientes*), fails, the author thinks, to make use of the basic concepts which determine the choices and force the student to discover the relevant generalizations on his own. The learner is working only with surface distinctions and, as a consequence, does not apprehend the controlling factors for adjective position. Performing the clause transformation, then noting the pause signal, the student executes two "extra" steps, which will not necessarily guarantee the development of the required intuition or a correct selection based on it.

Instead, Moody prefers to attack the problem directly by equipping the learner with the information he needs to make the decisions. In this case the information concerns the Spanish mathematical organization of reality as given by William Bull [See No. 5, pp. 214-231].

Even though the author sees Cressey's approach as dealing only with sounds and forms (this is arguable), he does not reject the use of transformation pattern drills which teach problem areas other than those that deal with semantic conditioning. He would accept Cressey's proposals for teaching the derivation of adjectives from adjective clauses after the student has internalized the basic concepts and overcome the difficulties of managing vocabulary in drills of up to twelve syllables.

Moody finally gets to his own strategy, which calls for explanation followed by drills of various types designed to connect the concepts to adjective position. The initial drills, about sixty sentences spread over two or three weeks, should be in English. The last step presents the problem to the student in personally meaningful ways, through questions based on sentences containing descriptive adjectives, whose position the learner must decide upon for a particular contextual usage. Another device (really a test) is a set of sentences with numbered points for the insertion of an adjective given in parentheses: *Mi* ₁ *suegra* ₂ *cocina muy bien* (*gordísma*). Based on the experiences of 2000 beginning students at Indiana University, "this procedure," we are assured, "really works."

64. NEWMAN, SAMUEL W.
"Audio-lingualism and the Reversibles," *Hisp*, 46 (May, 1963), 461-462.

Offers a grammar-translation type of aproach to the teaching of *gustar* even to audiolingual students. The author's techniques for teaching this troublesome verb involve these steps.

1) Students are exposed to *gustar*, via dialog or other sentences requiring memorization.

2) *Gustar* is explained in English to mean "to be pleasing."

3) Begin every translation for *gustar* with English *to*, e.g., "I like him" = "To me he is pleasing."

4) Repeat the prepositional phrase containing the pronoun. "I like eggs" > "To me to me are pleasing the eggs."

5) *Gustar* sentences are divided into two separate units. "I like him" = "To me to me // is pleasing (he)."

The author suggests the practicality of having the students in the early stages form the habit of using *a* for all sentences with *gustar*, even though not all *gustar* sentences require *a*. Newman sees this as oversimplification, rather than falsification of the language, and his experience has convinced him that this approach to the verb will help the students remember the basic parts of the correct sentence. He is not concerned that some sentences will sound overly emphatic. The author is on solid ground if the base sentence he advocates is in fact the underlying form, with deletion of *a* when called for. Others have agreed with this analysis and applied its assumptions in the materials and procedures of the classroom.

Newman offers other suggestions to facilitate the learning of *gustar*. He rightly urges the teacher to try to counteract the student's natural inclination to pluralize *gustar* when preceded by the plural pronoun (**les gustan cantar*).

All but the very inexperienced teacher know by now that no ready solutions exist for problematic *gustar* and many other difficult points which must be learned. But this does not mean that there exists no best approach or, more likely, combination of approaches to minimize the student's learning task.

65. RICHMAN, STEPHEN
"The Translation to Spanish of English Nouns in Juxtaposition,"
Hisp, 52 (September, 1969), 426-430.

Studies the particular problem of negative transfer into Spanish of the English noun modified by noun pattern. Whether the student simply translates directly from English (*tomato juice > tomate jugo*) or applies the Spanish word-order rule for descriptive adjectives (*tomato juice > jugo tomate*), he can, unless he is aware of the lexical and structural differences, produce unacceptable word sequences.

To prevent or at least minimize the learning problem, the author suggests that the instructor first call attention to the general problem of interference and pointedly spell out the devices Spanish employs to render the English noun-noun combinations. These could be introduced one by one and in order of importance.

Richman describes, with examples, six different lexical formulae used in Spanish to translate the noun-noun constituent:

1) **Spanish noun + noun** (rare): *papel carbón, lengua madre*, with the modifying noun second.

2) **Noun + adjective.** Although Spanish nouns rarely function adjectivally, they often have related adjectival forms: *correo aéreo, año escolar.* The problem for the student, is, of course, knowing if the needed adjective exists, and, if it does not, how to produce the information another way.

3) **Noun + *de* + noun.** This is the majority combination, with the last two words serving as a modifying phrase to the first noun: *libro de español, sala de espera.* Because of its high frequency the rule for this pattern should be generalized and heavily practiced. The *de* + **infinitive** variation (*máquina de escribir*) is also included.

4) **Noun + *para* + noun.** In most cases the modifying noun expresses the purpose of the principal noun: *cepillo para el pelo, píldoras para dormir*, though Spanish will not always use *para* when purpose is implied: *lavadora* for *washing machine.*

5) **Noun.** Often one Spanish noun translates two in English: *ice cream > helado, flower shop > florería.* The author correctly observes that many of these English expressions are written as one noun (*mailbox, fingernail*, etc.), but that this is of no structural interest since it is strictly an orthographic matter.

6) **Verb + noun compounds.** Characteristic of Spanish are a considerable number of verb-noun units, for which Richman takes the noun to be direct object of the verb element: *abrecartas, lavacoches.* The author separates his examples into conceptual groups. This structure is all but nonexistent in English.

Richman sympathizes with the student in that he will not be able to predict which of these six patterns to use, but once he has learned to rid his Spanish of all noun-noun combinations and begun to store specific phrases, he can then use his feel for the language and apply, for example, formula 3, and meet with regular success.

66. SAPORTA, SOL
"Problems in the Comparison of the Morphemic Systems of English and Spanish," *Hisp*, 39 (March, 1956), 36-40.

The purpose of this paper is to identify some of the problems involved in comparing the morphemic systems of English and Spanish. Knowledge of the differences will serve to determine the selection, presentation and ordering of language materials. Three areas of comparison are treated: 1) When the corresponding elements are identical in every way, with no learning problems; 2) When a form in the native language diverges into two forms in the target language, with considerable difficulties for the learner (Engl. *but*, Span. *pero* and *sino*); and 3) When there is no analogous form in the native language (Span. personal *a*; the person marker of *cantas*), also a problem area. Supposedly no problem prevails for Spanish *de*, English *of* and *from*, with convergence in the target language, but it must be observed that the situation is not all that simple (cf. *desde*).

Saporta makes certain statements and leaves other implications about the nature of language learning which, while most representative of the thinking of the time, no longer reflect the author's beliefs. These remarks involve the role of analogy function, habit development, and cognitive learning. Regarding the latter, we are told that "there is no reason to assume that the ability to intellectualize or verbalize about Spanish is correlated with this [language] ability we are trying to develop."

The author also discusses probability of occurrence of morpheme sequences in terms of practice and habit formation. This and the other notions presented here are mostly familiar, but interesting for the perspective they evidence for the changing state of applied linguistics.

67. SCHMITZ, JOHN ROBERT
"The *Se Me* Construction: Reflexive for Unplanned Occurrences," *Hisp*, 49 (September, 1966), 430-433.

Commenting on Holton's [See No. 57] and Moen's [No. 61] findings regarding the relative order of direct and indirect object pronouns in

Spanish, Schmitz agrees with the exceptions they offer, when DO can precede IO pronouns. But he would follow the hierarchy of difficulty criteria suggested by Stockwell, Bowen and Martin [Refer to No. 70] to determine which low frequency usages to exclude from first- and second-year courses.

The author applauds the accuracy and usefulness of the rules given for the *se me/se le* reflexive for unplanned occurrences in *Modern Spanish* and elsewhere [for example, in Bull, No. 5, p. 267], but is not satisfied that constructions such as *se me subió la sangre*, or *se me hace agua la boca*, fall into the same category. Schmitz has combed hundreds of pages of mostly modern Spanish authors for similar examples of what he calls "involuntary physiological or emotional reactions," which he groups according to the part of the body involved.

In addition to events representing "unplanned occurrence," the author recommends a second category for the type just described and yet a third, for the reflexive with "figurative catastrophic events" (*se le viene encima*). He does not think that the label "unplanned occurrence" should be used to characterize all cases of the general pattern, since those of the second group are not accidental or non-premeditative, and the third type of event, while unplanned and even accidental, unlike category 1 cannot change from a deliberate to an accidental act (*Rompí el vaso* > *Se me rompió el vaso*).

Conceptually Schmitz perhaps has made valid distinctions, though grammatically he is dealing with only one structure. However, there is no reason why, as the author suggests, these patterns could or should not be drilled separately.

68. SCHNEER, RICHARD JAMES
"The Future and Conditional of Probability—A Teaching Technique," *Hisp*, 43 (March, 1960), 148.

The author, finding textbook presentations of the non-systemic uses of Spanish future and conditional forms weak and confusing to his students, suggests a technique which pinpoints the signals for the occurrence of these forms.

He recommends first bracketing the "I wonder," "you suppose," or "probably" segments of the English sentence. This bracketed information indicates that the corresponding Spanish utterance will contain the future or conditional morphemes. The second step is to translate the English version minus the words in brackets, then supply the correct time (the same) and order markers. [*I wonder*] *where John has been.* > *¿Dónde ha estado Juan?* > *¿Dónde habrá estado Juan?*

By calling the student's attention to the conjecture or probability idea and specifically training the student to anticipate the appearance of the future and conditional morphemes, he will be less likely to seek non-verbal equivalents. Schneer could go one step further in his analysis and presentation and establish the separate functions of the time and order markers he is discussing.

As for acceptable translations of the Spanish, the author guides his students by telling them that only context can determine the appropriate English version.

69. SEELYE, H. NED
    "The Spanish Passive: A Study in the Relation Between Linguistic Form and World-View," *Hisp*, 49 (May, 1966), 290-292.

Questions the accuracy of the "commonly stated" textbook description which holds that the Spanish speaker uses the passive voice to detach himself from the "reality" (*sic*) with which he views his involvement. "Whereas the Anglo makes things happen, the Latino has things happen to him." Seelye drew up a questionnaire in an effort to determine what basis, if any, exists for this belief.

Specifically, the author attempted to find out what conditions the native's choice, when he has one, between the active and the passive. The questionnaire presented six contrasting situations for which the respondent was asked to supply one form or the other. Three factors were stressed: 1) subject emphasis, 2) feelings of responsibility, and 3) role. The questionnaire underwent three revisions (based on reactions of native speakers) before it was administered to fifty educated Guatemalans.

Findings: Even when the subject of conversation was strongly emphasized, no clear choice was discerned. The surrounding verbal context appeared to override the element of emphasis. The passive was not used to evade guilt or deny personal responsibility. But situations involving fatalism and import elicited 30 percent more passives, though reasons for the preferences are not clear. When the individual (1st person) was directly involved in the action, the active was preferred.

This kind of study can be very illuminating in apprehending patterns of usage. However, because of the variables operating in this investigation it is not surprising that more consistency was not maintained by the respondents. Certainly relationships do exist between linguistic form and what the author calls "world-view," and his modest survey seeks this kind of very useful information.

70. STOCKWELL, ROBERT P., J. DONALD BOWEN
    and JOHN W. MARTIN
    The Grammatical Structures of English and Spanish. (Contrastive
    Structure Series.) Chicago and London: The University of
    Chicago Press, 1965. xi + 328 pp.

This study of the similarities and differences between the grammars of
English and Spanish is a companion volume to Stockwell and Bowen's *The
Sounds of English and Spanish* [No. 35]. Whereas the volumes in the
Contrastive Structure Series which study sound systems may claim a
degree of completeness, those on grammar treat only selected topics.
Nonetheless, other than Bull's investigation [See No. 5] this is the only
comprehensive presentation available of the pedagogical problems in
teaching the grammar of Spanish to English-speaking learners. And,
fortunately for the teacher and the researcher, the book under
consideration offers different information and some different approaches.
   The primary purpose of this study is to outline the various areas of
conflict between the structures of the native and the target languages.
Contrastive analysis is used to point out, in a way that the non-linguist can
understand, where the two languages overlap and diverge. In highlighting
especially the latter, the authors have endeavored to show where, how, and
to what degree learning interference is likely to take place. Throughout the
book they cite "typical errors," supposedly caught on the fly. And all
language examples were authenticated by consultation with educated
native speakers. Doubtless many native speakers would reject some of the
Spanish phrases and sentences, or at least would not readily find a context
for them.
   Contents, with an indication of primary writing responsibility for each
chapter:
   (1) Introduction to grammatical analysis (R.P.S.)
   (2) Basic sentence patterns (R.P.S.)
   (3) Word classes and morphological characteristics (J.D.B.)
   (4) The noun phrase and its constituents (J.D.B.)
   (5) Verb forms (J.D.B.)
   (6) The auxiliary constituents of the verb phrase (R.P.S. and
       J.W.M.)
   (7) Other constituents of the verb phrase (J.D.B., R.P.S. and
       J.W.M.)
   (8) Simple sentence transformations (R.P.S.)
   (9) Complex and compound sentence transformations (R.P.S.)

(10) Lexical differences (J.W.M.)

(11) Hierarchy of difficulty (R.P.S.)

Chapter 1 contains good statements on what grammar is and is not. Chapter 2 presents for the first time an inventory of the basic sentence patterns of Spanish, alongside those of English. The theoretical foundation is that of the generative concept of grammar. In the chapter on word and morpheme classes the reader follows a mostly structural development and so also for Chapter 4 on the noun phrase and its constituents. The approach in this particular chapter is most inconsonant with that of the others, which derive from Chomsky's view of language. The sections on verbs are insightful and admirably complete, given the scope of the undertaking.

The last chapter attempts to sum up the author's findings in terms of pedagogical implications. Specifically, they advance the notion of a hierarchy of difficulty, which depends for its validity on the assumption that some correspondences are more difficult to learn than others. Such a hierarchy, according to the authors, is a set of predictions which can only be tested in the classroom by the linguistically sophisticated teacher, upon whom devolves the kinds of corroborated information sought in this study. Mostly theoretical bases are used to establish a list of correspondences, ordered from most to least difficult to master. But other categories of interference are included in the system. The resulting hierarchy list is not as complete as the one found in the companion volume on sounds, but it is at the least, interesting and potentially of considerable promise for future materials writers. [For a somewhat skeptical assessment of this approach, see Sol Saporta's review of this volume in *Hisp*, 50 (March, 1967), 199-200.]

This study was in the making before a transformational grammar of Spanish had even seen its beginning. The authors embrace this theory as the soundest one for contrastive study, but it is not surprising that considerable eclecticism pervades (and for some, weakens) their collaboration. However, in their Preface they acknowledge how much more useful their efforts could have been, had a complete transformational grammar of Spanish been available. Many of their formulations must be taken as no more than tenuous suggestions and they readily admit that teachers and researchers alike must pool their resources if possession of comparative studies realized in explicit terms is ever to become an accomplished fact.

Stockwell, Bowen and Martin's work is not a definitive study, but it is an important one. Their ideas have been the springboard for many of the articles found in these pages.

71. WILSON, ROBERT E.
"Polite Ways to Give Orders," *Hisp*, 48 (March, 1965), 117-118.

A note on the often overlooked use of the present indicative to express the idea of "please" in Spanish. While learning to manipulate the subjunctive and imperative verb forms is useful to the student, he should also become acquainted with the other ways Spanish speakers give commands and voice requests.

Whether or not it is the case that "most Spanish-speaking people usually give orders in the plain present indicative," this use of the indicative is indeed common, and, as the author explains, especially when there is no conflict with the familiar imperative (*"Me trae un vaso de agua, por favor,"* but not **"Trae un vaso de agua, por favor"*). This pattern would normally take a slightly rising inflection, though not as much as for the yes-no question. The purpose and the result is a half-question, half-request which the speaker chooses instead of the subjunctive command which, depending on the context, might sound too formal or too brusque.

Another way of sending the same kind of softened command is the redundant use of the subject pronoun. The indicative, either second or third person, singular or plural, can substitute for the direct command, providing that either an object pronoun or a subject pronoun precedes the verb.

Wilson also points out the Mexican construction *Favor de* + infinitive and *Me hace el favor de* + infinitive. Also, *Sírva(n)se* + infinitive.

Although concentrating on the subject of the "please" expressions in Spanish, this article is also a more general statement on linguistic appropriateness. Students are taught one or several ways to express an idea in Spanish, but their Spanish too often does not include yet other ways of saying the same thing, or, more importantly, the student will not know when to use what, since his command of what he has learned is limited to a general or a classroom context. In other words, his sentence may seem perfectly grammatical out of context, but not when heard in actual conversation; he simply cannot make native speaker discriminations of this kind.

IV. Listening and Speaking

72. ANTOINE, GERALDINE
" 'Conversational Spanish'—A One Year High School Course,"
Hisp, 55 (December, 1972), 891-893.

Describes a one-year experimental course designed to offer a basic speaking knowledge of Spanish to high school students. The *La Familia Fernández* film-text materials were used with 18 students. Grammar was noted only to correct speech. The approach to an expanded vocabulary was topical. In keeping with an increased use of introductory listening comprehension practice, the films were shown and followed by question/answer sessions.

Though the stated objectives of the course were the oral skills, reading and writing were used to reinforce what had been learned orally. And there seems to have been a heavy reliance on various kinds of visual aids, mainly teacher-produced.

The language lab was used twice a week. Some form of review was held during each class. Testing was mainly oral, with frequent daily quizzes. Antoine judged the progress through the lessons quite rapid and, instead of the usual attrition, the class size actually increased. It would be difficult to assess the apparent student enthusiasm, presumably higher than for the usual high school classes taught by this same instructor. Perhaps it was a result of merely getting away from grammar rules, or of increased student oral participation. Or simply the particular chemistry of this group of students, or the idea that the class was different, experimental. Most likely the success was due to a combination of these factors.

At any rate, conversational Spanish was added to the permanent curriculum of this high school.

73. KALIVODA, THEODORE B.
"An Individual Study Course for Facilitating Advanced Oral Skills," *MLJ*, 56 (December, 1972), 492-495.

Outlines an individual study procedure intended to provide advanced oral training in addition to the usual departmental course offerings. Needed to implement the intensive contact lessons are a taped program, a monolingual (Spanish) dictionary and a tape recorder.

Learning activity involves two phases: listening, then speaking. Phase I consists of sections on vocabulary, lesson content and questions. The words chosen for dictation are limited to "extraordinary," meaning troublesome vocabulary. The sequence: 1) the Spanish word; 2) the English translation; 3) a spelling in the FL; 4) an optional repetition; and finally 5) the word in a short context. Next follows the lesson content, a narration or a dialog – ordinary colloquial, or "street" Spanish is recommended. The idea is to balance the commonly deliberate language of the average classroom. Sources of usable materials are suggested. The third and final step of Phase I is a series of oral questions, given only once, and for which, ultimately, one hundred percent correct responses are required. The author suggests that the students submit written responses as well.

The second stage, which Kalivoda acknowledges as falling short of actual talk, requires the student to deliver on tape or in the class an oral summary of the listening lesson.

Writing is only minimally involved, and then mainly for corroboration. Since little time is required for supervision the teacher burdened with too many back-to-back classes can manage some free time to better pace his energies. At the college level these procedures could either replace regular classes or afford homework practice. The requirement of intensive concentration (several hours daily for college students) is noted as possibly unpopular and, thus, a weakness in the program.

For many teachers who adopt this or similar course structures the resulting inventory of reusable lessons compensates for the large initial outlay of work.

Any teacher or coordinator who chooses this approach will be familiar with the arguments for and against programs which place less emphasis on contact with the live teacher.

74. NACCI, CHRIS N.
     "Enriching the Audio-lingual Activity in the Classroom," *Hisp*, 48 (March, 1965), 109-114.

The specific recommendation made here is that the audiolingual student spend most of his time answering graded questions. The suggested pace of the class is as intense and quick as the teacher can maintain it, and this can be accomplished only by an instructor who is well prepared and in complete control of the class at all times. Furthermore, the teacher must be convinced that the possible negative effects of the frenzied pace will be offset by positive results. Nacci's experience is that this kind of practice works because it is pedagogically sound and affords each student maximum participation (perhaps averaging ten answers a session) with minimum self-consciousness.

The author begins this activity with the twenty-fifth 50-minute class of the beginning and intermediate courses. As a result, the first year students answer some 10,000 questions, those of the second year, about 5,000, by the cut-off point at the middle of the second semester.

The questions, based on the usual topical material, are graded so that the learner can or should be able to give spontaneous, correct answers, usually based on previous questions and answers. He begins with simple *Sí, sé que...* answers, which require no additions or changes other than *¿Sabe?* to *Sí, sé,* and, of course, the appropriate intonation. From this he proceeds through a series of other kinds of (usually information) questions until he attains the ability to answer the most involved questions, i.e., *¿Por qué?, ¿Qué cree?,* etc. There is much to be said for this buildup technique, for it implies a hierarchy of difficulty based on linguistic structure. These same kinds of questions can readily be personalized, and the whole operation, unlike that of pattern drills (which this in some ways is), becomes less mechanical and approaches actual communication.

One application of this rapid-fire question-answer activity is in testing. Though rather difficult to use for objective measurement, the teacher can nevertheless judge proficiency levels as based on literally hundreds of answers by each student. These answers can of course be recorded on tape if the teacher experiences difficulty in grading answers fired back at him at so fast a pace.

Instead of continuing this activity past the midpoint of the second semester, Nacci prefers that the student begin to participate in "normal conversation" based on materials thoroughly prepared outside of class. This is done entirely in Spanish and could include individual recitation in groups of 3 to 5 students. The teacher evaluates, guides and motivates.

Nacci concludes his article with an outline of integrated activities including practice of all four language skills. The author requires (and presumably gets) two hours of preparation by the student for every hour spent in class.

Whether or not a teacher will accept this approach to mastering comprehension and speaking will depend on his theory of learning and his specific goals. And while all teachers recognize that the student's training must go beyond answering questions in the FL few challenge the question-answer technique as an effective teaching tool, perhaps at all levels of learning.

75. RYAN, JAMES
 "Spanish Composition and Conversation," *Hisp*, 44 (May, 1961), 297-301.

Discusses the problems encountered in the intermediate or advanced course in Spanish composition. Ryan follows Robert G. Mead's definition of composition, which calls for "idiomatic expression, *orally* or *in writing*, of ideas in a proper syntactical frame." Besides free composition and liberated oral expression, the author would also include intermediate steps of translation, expansion drills, answering questions, oral or written résumés of reading material.

The first question is that of materials. The author does not use a review grammar for this type of course, but allows that it can be profitably used in addition to other texts. Advocated are lessons stressing the finer points of Spanish grammar, and for which are useful various types of word and idiom lists. These materials should include readings based on everyday Hispanic life and made up of practical and not too difficult vocabulary.

Ryan is right in maintaining that it is the teacher and the tasks the students are asked to perform—not the textbook(s)—which spell success or failure for the course in composition and conversation. It is fine that he doesn't push use of a review grammar, and even better that he points out the merits of interesting *revista* materials. But fortunately, in addition to these, the teacher now has considerably more choice if he decides to use a text which does contain some or much grammar and lexical review. Since the more recent introductory and intermediate grammars tend to include fewer grammar points (for example, the past subjunctive is no longer thought to be necessary for a "complete" first-year text), the level of actual linguistic competence assumed by Ryan might be too much beyond the appropriate focus of post-fourth-course study. Thus, the teacher would want to present those grammar points and lexical groups known not to have been covered during the previous instruction. Good articulation of sequent courses is, of course, a must.

Classroom guidelines: 1) No English permitted in class, the offender to be "punished;" 2) Oral exercises to include reading aloud, answering questions (both prepared and spontaneous), résumés and brief speeches (impromptu and prepared); 3) Individual work, including one special oral assignment a week, though with total class involvement the norm; 4) Oral and written work combined in the "composition" course, since they go hand in hand; 5) Written translation from English into Spanish; 6) Written expansion drills, ending with almost uncued, free composition; 7) Tape-recorded samples to demonstrate oral progress; 8) No over-emphasis of vocabulary building, though the student should be trained to use the dictionary; 9) Discussion and illustration of the nature of composition and how to outline a topic; 10) Grading should not be on the basis of mistakes alone.

76. SEGREDA, WILLIAM and ALBERT VALDMAN
   "Teaching Spoken Spanish in High School and College," *Hisp*, 44 (May, 1961), 375-381.

Participation in an NDEA Institute as applied linguist and methodologist led to the authors' collaboration in this article which studies the issues of dialogs, drills and free conversation. Writing in 1961, when audiolingual practices were just becoming widespread, Segreda and

Valdman ask this not rhetorical or unimportant question, which we can now answer: "Can the audio-lingual approach ... be adapted to the average college or high school situation where classes of thirty or more students meet for three, four, or five hours per week?" Successful adaptation is implied, of course, and some ten years and literally thousands of classes oriented towards the goals and procedures discussed here have yielded the clear verdict that too many in the profession were guilty of expecting the impossible of this new methodology. No consolation to those less-than-successful students were the early and repeated cautions in the literature voicing skepticism as to the workability of the audiolingual approach, especially for large classes (not to mention untrained teachers and poor materials and lab programs).

Very revealing and quite accurate is the calculation that in a class of five students each student could theoretically perform (orally in audiolingual classes) for ten minutes, vs. only two minutes in a large average class. Why then should it have come as a surprise to the disappointed teacher to realize that his student never learned to express himself in Spanish after one or two or three or more semesters of conscientious audiolingual training!

The authors assume that classes will be large and therefore attempt to describe mainly those in-class procedures which can overcome the handicap of oversize. These suggestions, based on the FSI ("guided imitation") method, include: 1) The teacher should at all times use his own best judgement in pacing the class, allowing certain overlearning and not feeling obligated to cover all the patterns of the language; 2) New (dialog) sentences should be introduced at less than normal speaking speed, while preserving the phonological features of conversational style; 3) Too much emphasis should not be given to intonation problems; 4) Since not all features of the language are of equal importance at any linguistic level, the student will best practice the key elements and especially those of the target language which vary most from the native tongue. More emphasis on inflection than on word order; 5) To obtain maximum participation of each student, individual repetition should be kept to a minimum, with choral response heavily used. For some drills choral response can be the echo version of the individual recitation, permitting performance of each drill sentence by all students; 6) Class groups of ten to fifteen students for repetition of the dialog, with spot checking for individual problems; 7) Balance of individual and class practice with directed (expanded) dialog work and free conversation; 8) As for reading and writing (with "subordination of these two derived skills"), their role is to be viewed as supportive. Dictations (for comprehension), translation drills, and reading of graded materials complement the other activities of the program.

These suggestions are sound for the class of any size. The questionable points are those involving relative emphasis on intonation, the written skills, individual practice.

V. Reading and Writing

77. BEBERFALL, LESTER
"A Note on the *Nuevas Normas de Prosodia y Ortografía*
(1959)," *Hisp*, 45 (September, 1962), 504-508.

Observations on the Spanish Royal Academy's 1959 "nuevas normas de
prosodia y ortografía" (12ªb), with special attention to the use of the
written accent involving diphthongs. The author first demonstrates the
familiar, time-tested rule which governs the placement of the written
accent mark on Spanish words determined by the specific letter with
which the word ends (including those words which are exceptions to the
general rule and which require the written diacritic to identify the actual
stressed syllable). Beberfall commends the decisions of the Academy in
that practically all the rules are based on objective criteria which produce
consistent patterns of usage. This consistency includes the diphthong
situations and those would-be diphthongs (*país, baúl, día, continúa*) which
are not, because the normally "weak" *u* and *i* replace "strong" *a, o* or *e* as
the strong stressed (and so indicated) of the adjacent vowels.
It is fine that the monosyllables *fui, fue, dio, vio,* etc. no longer carry
the written stress, since the second element in the diphthong is stressed,
but the author is bothered that a word like *guión* must still be marked for
stress. True, the Academy did not reveal all its guidelines in appearing to
establish two different rules for similar (and even identical) phonological
segments, but Beberfall has failed to deduce the obvious reasoning of the
rule makers; namely, that since *fui, dio,* etc. are so frequent in occurrence
and are known to all who read Spanish, the written accent is redundant. In
attempting to show that the sequence *ui* does not constitute a diphthong
when the first vowel takes the primary stress, *flúido*, for example, is
incorrectly syllabicated: *flú-i-do.*
The author omits other examples of changes made by the 1959 rules
intended to simplify and clarify use of the stress marker.
Though not an entirely comprehensive nor particularly satisfying
interpretation of the Academy's spelling rules, most of the information is
accurate and should help the teacher understand the problems involved.
The article does provide the basic facts behind the summarized textbook
versions of the rules for the written accent. [See No. 84 for a more
thorough discussion of the orthographic accent and the principles which
govern its use.]

78. BLAYNE, THORNTON C.
"Results of Developmental Reading Procedures in First-Year
Spanish," *MLJ*, 30 (January, 1946), 39-43.

The author wanted to find out if methods of improving reading comprehension in English could be used effectively in developing reading ability in a FL. Another question involved the optimum point in the beginning class to introduce these procedures.

Blayne presents the results of an experimental tryout of developmental reading techniques with a group of seventeen first-year high school Spanish students. [An analysis of the methods used, together with a sample unit, is to be found in the author's article, "Building Comprehension in Silent Reading," *MLJ*, 29 (April, 1945), 270-276.] At the end of a year's study of Spanish, these students were reading an average 315 words per minute with 90 percent comprehension of graded material. This reading rate approximates that for speed of comprehension in reading English. Five students actually exceeded the norm for reading ability in English. The entire group demonstrated control considerably above the oral reading rates in English (about 175 words per minute), which meant they were not vocalizing individual words.

Though considerable irregularity is seen in the progress graph for selected high, median and low-ranking achievers, the general trend is upward. Explanations are given for the uneven growth curves.

The methodology: 1) Early introduction of special training in silent reading; 2) Emphasis on reading for *ideas* rather than for words; 3) Guided practice in silent reading apart from oral reading work; 4) Instruction in the objectives and methods of the program; 5) Continuous evaluation; 6) Appealing reading materials; 7) Gradual but imperceptible increase in difficulty of selections and tests; and 8) "Psychologically" spaced practice.

Blayne does not advocate this kind of practice as a substitute for either translation or other kinds of "careful, detailed work." Nor does he believe that reading units cannot (later) be used for oral drill.

One must question, however, the advisability of utilizing any kind of speed-reading techniques and practice, especially during the first year of FL study, for in many students it tends to encourage sloppy habits. What are careless oral responses doubtless assume even more communication blur when the student has only himself to monitor his performance.

79. BOWEN, J. DONALD and ROBERT P. STOCKWELL
    "Orthography and Respelling in Teaching Spanish," *Hisp*, 40 (May, 1957), 200-205.

Reopens the discussion of the usefulness of respelling in teaching Spanish. Bowen and Stockwell can see no good reason why a pedagogical respelling, which would differ from the conventional one at critical points, could not be used to advantage, even though by their own admission

Spanish orthography ranks high on a one-to-one correspondence scale for phonemic representation. They advocate a separate transcription mainly because of the deceptively familiar Roman alphabet and the resulting trouble spots, many of which involve interference from English.

The authors list typical student pronunciation problems which persist regardless of how the Spanish is spelled: /ř/, /p,t,k/ (because of the aspiration), certain consonant clusters, vowel reduction, and the like. Other types of mistakes are induced by the traditional orthography or because the spelling gives the learner no clue as to what phonetic value(s) he should produce. For example, spelling hides the two allophones of Spanish /d/, and similarly, of /b,g,s/. Bowen and Stockwell do not accept the argument that simple distributional rules will suffice. The first stages of exposure to the sounds can be made less troublesome, they feel, if respelling is used to cue proper responses.

Other reasons for adopting this system for Spanish include phonological reduction (*Va a hablar*) and all the prosodic features (pitch, juncture, stress) not signaled by the orthography. This last group constitutes perhaps the author's strongest argument.

We are told that a respelling period will not cause difficulty when the student begins to read from actual spelling. Writing is another matter, however, and, as is pointed out, the learner will recall the symbols he has been using in the transcriptions.

That teachers and materials writers have not adopted respelling as a pedagogical device is due to their conviction that it represents an unnecessary intermediate step. The teacher who would place considerable importance on accurate spelling might be willing to take the extra time needed to introduce a respelling.

80. CALVERT, LAURA
    "The Role of Written Exercises in an Audio-lingual Program,"
    Hisp, 48 (May, 1965), 313-316.

Proposes the use of certain written exercises, first developed in a Peace Corps program, in regular university courses. The author is careful to mention the significant differences which would ordinarily distinguish Peace Corps trainees from students at the college level. She has a good understanding of these variables and believes the two groups hold enough in common to similarly learn from a given approach--here the utilization of "the written word for all it is worth."

Calvert treads opaque water in discussing the visual symbol as an aid to memory and an advantage in drilling. The argument that written work is something the learner can do by himself is not the strongest. Nor a substitute to spell endless oral drill, other than in intensive programs, such as the Peace Corps, in which the student will end most days exhausted no matter what. On the other hand, the author recognizes the firm interfering visual orientation of most adult learners and the bad pronunciation habits that result from seeing the written symbols too soon.

As an example of combining visual and aural perception for reinforcement, Calvert describes the use of cards containing the individual verb morphemes, which first serve as the total model for practice, but then are removed one by one until the student is forced to rely on memory alone. Other kinds of written exercises, designed mainly to overcome the handicap of limited study time at home, were employed in presenting vocabulary and the grammar. A fast pace was maintained at all times, as written work can tend to slow down the class.

One would question the author's view that oral exercises only rarely can be used as written drills, and, further, the implication that they must be substantially different in format if they are to take advantage of visual retention. And a statement such as "We have found overt teaching of grammar principles to be more efficient than reliance on induction," is open to many questions. Principally, more efficient in what way? how determined? and on what comparative basis?

But in general the kinds of written exercises described here and an account of the relationships to their oral drill counterparts are valid. And the teacher is warned to be on the lookout for those desperate eye-minded students who would tenaciously hold on to the textbook, but who must be gently but surely weaned from the written crutch.

81. CARSELLO, CARMEN J. and LUCILLE V. BRAUN
    "Rapid Reading Spanish Material," *MLJ*, 56 (March, 1972), 148-150.

Following on a similar study for Portuguese at the University of Illinois, Chicago Circle, this report details the results of an experiment among graduate students designed to test the feasibility of teaching rapid reading. The eight language majors were about equally divided among native and nonnative speakers of Spanish, but all had a firm command of the grammar and mostly did not consult dictionaries in their reading.

The participants spent some twenty hours in the reading laboratory, in addition to their regular seminar (in Galdós). Initial reading rates were determined for both narrative and "study" materials, using the McGraw-Hill and Nelson Denny Reading tests. The students were instructed in the rapid reading process via lectures and special study materials before they began to work with narrative and text passages (from Galdós' works and critical essays about them).

The results demonstrated that all students made significant progress in increasing their rates of reading all materials used, both Spanish and English. The only area in which little rate increase showed up was for the nonnatives reading English text (literature) and Spanish critical essay material. The native increased his rates in both languages and for all types of passages.

With only eight participants, the sample is, as the authors rightly acknowledge, too small for any solid proof of advantages in rapid reading techniques or of significant differences between native and nonnative readers. The results do, however, suggest further experimentation.

82. NACCI, CHRIS N.
   "Realizing the Reading Comprehension and Literature Aims via an Audio-lingual Orientation," *Hisp*, 49 (May, 1966), 274-281.

To ascertain the level of difficulty of some 100 plays, novels and collections of short stories read in introductory literature courses at the University of Akron, students indicated for each: 1) the total time spent in preparation, 2) the degree of language difficulty, 3) how interesting the text was, and 4) where and why the students stopped reading, if they did not finish the book. These easy-to-difficult and degree-of-interest ratings enable the teachers to guide the students through as many of the texts as possible, with greater efficiency and enthusiasm.

Nacci reports that the students agreed after completing the courses that they were reading faster in Spanish than in English. This was accomplished by having the student:

1) Read whole sentences instead of words;

2) Use context as clues to lexical meanings, rather than looking them up in the dictionary;

3) Avoid translation;

4) Time himself to know that he was reading more each day; and

5) Read the easier books first.

All of this reading is intended to nourish conversation, as well as fulfill the other goals of a course in literature. Wholehearted utilization of the audiolingual approach is found to allow the realization of all the traditional course aims. Students talk in Spanish during the entire period; they are divided into seminar groups in which each student expresses his reactions and observations regarding what he has read. This, in turn, brings out opinions, amplifications and clarifications from the other students.

Since rarely do any two students read the same work, one might fear that this free conversation become a one-role dialog. And the whole approach assumes a firm oral command of the language by all the participants.

The teachers rightly choose to begin with contemporary readings. Their argument is that the conventional introduction to literature through the Medieval, Renaissance, Golden Age, etc., periods will not lend itself to fostering an atmosphere of communication between the students. That the student's reading should serve to improve his command of Spanish is never lost sight of.

The instructor is an active participant in each seminar group; his role is to listen, guide, motivate and add to what is said in class. He equips himself with a checklist of grammar points to use in pinpointing the weaknesses of individual students, but this continuous "grading" cannot be obtrusive. Nacci describes a range of techniques he has used to insure success for his students. So convinced is he of the effectiveness of this approach that he does not hesitate to pair his best students with native speakers, with the requirement that the American must make so few mistakes in language that he not pain the native, that he communicate the content and spirit of his reading with ease, and that the native's contributions be fully understood by the nonnative.

83. OLSTAD, CHARLES
    "Composition in Imitation," *Hisp*, 47 (May, 1964), 452-454.

An approach to advanced composition based on the imitation of literary models. [This concept is carried out in the author's (with Leo L. Barrow) textbook, *Creative Spanish*. New York: Harper and Row, 1965. A similar treatment is to be found in the very successful text by Paul C. Smith and Cándido Ayllón, *Spanish Composition through Literature*. Englewood Cliffs, N.J.: Prentice-Hall, Inc., 1968.] Olstad sketches his own application of this not new principle in a step-by-step procedure, which he employed in third-year composition classes at the University of Arizona:

1) Students read for comprehension dittoed selections of representative prose authors. This involves translation into English, with a discussion of alternative possibilities. To insure a better understanding, the teacher can prepare a series of notes explaining words and expressions.

2) Style (understood in the broadest sense) is discussed, including a consideration of individual words, images, syntax, the author's point of view and approach, etc.

3) The student's own first efforts in writing. Olstad finds it best to begin this step first in class, with a discussion of possible topics. The teacher's job is to give direction and form to the student's ideas and imagination, or to the learner's reactions to those of the teacher—in other words, a useful orientation.

4) The student next prepares either a careful outline or a completed composition. Needless to say, the student is to incorporate into his composition those points of grammar and features of style characteristic of the model he is imitating.

5) The finished compositions may be read in class, with follow-up discussion.

The author cautions that outright plagiarism is inevitable, but that this should not disconcert the instructor since it can benefit especially the weak student in the first weeks. Just as often, hopefully, the teacher will admire the results of a serious original effort. At times the compositions will betray a heavy reliance on the dictionary, with misapplication. But skilled use of the dictionary (including perhaps a dictionary of synonyms) is one of the objectives. Too, there will be those more "original" students who prefer to create on their own, rather than follow the literary model, but who end up with bad Spanish, because they have gone beyond the control of their linguistic competence, or with banal ideas. The teacher should decide the amount of freedom needed by each student.

Olstad reproduces a rather good composition by a student who lacked imagination and literary talent, and who "could scarcely utter a correct Spanish sentence." He suggests that this student at least had learned considerable vocabulary, additional knowledge (but surely not control) of the grammar, and even a feeling for Bécquer's poetic prose. To be questioned is the advisability, even at the third-year level, of concentrating on imitation of literary models when the student has not yet attained an acceptable degree of colloquial oral fluency. Not that practice of one cannot improve the other.

84. SACKS, NORMAN P.
"The Pattern Drill and the Rationale of the Prosodic and Orthographic Accents in Spanish," *Hisp*, 46 (May, 1963), 361-372.

A study of the Spanish orthographic accent, as related to problems of prosodic stress [See No. 33 for author's fuller treatment of the latter]. In general Sacks finds the traditional textbook rules for written accentuation accurate and clear. The author's purpose is to refine and restate these rules in terms of certain structural features of Spanish, to point out the rationale behind their development, and to suggest appropriate drills to help the student form sound writing habits.

Sacks' correct premise is that the orthographic accent should be approached via the language's stress patterns. He gives five principles: 1) In Spanish the written accent enables us to determine the stressed syllable for all words where spelling (the rule) does not (the exception) give us this information. In Spanish, unlike English, the location of the stressed syllable of the written word is obvious in all cases. 2) Most Spanish words carry stress on the penult syllable; the majority of the remainder are stressed on the last syllable. Exceptions to these require the orthographic accent on the stressed vowel. 3) The placement of stress and written accents in Spanish are determined by three vowels (*a,e,o*) and six consonants (*d,l,r,z,n,s*). 4) Spanish words, with or without written accents, with very few exceptions are stressed on the same syllables as the Latin words from which they are derived. 5) The rules on the use of the orthographic accent in Spanish have historically been determined by three principles: economy, consistency and analogy.

Demonstrating "how the principles of economy of effort, consistency, and analogy have operated, sometimes in conflict, in determining the use of the orthographic accent," the author shows, for example, why because of pattern Spanish words that end in -*s* (mostly plurals) and -*n* (usually verbs) do not follow the stress rule for words ending in the other consonants. The Academy's changing rules (as early as 1885) are seen to favor economy, then consistency, then full circle back to economy—the two principles operating in conflict. The role of analogy is also discussed.

Sacks offers his own version of a complete set of rules for the written accent. Even though all of these rules are necessary to any full treatment of the problem, the author realizes that textbook versions have justifiably abbreviated the information. There is a further discussion of the minority patterns. All of the rules and observations follow from the author's five general principles.

Attention is next turned to the application of these principles and rules to the teaching of Spanish stress, using pattern practice. Since effective pattern drills can be devised to teach correct phonological, morphological and syntactical habits, Sacks believes that pattern practice can profitably be extended to include the writing skill. The balance of the author's paper is devoted to suggested pattern practice on Spanish stress and accent (with an understanding of the underlying principles). Working in analogous groups, the author utilizes minimal pairs and other contrastive patterns. He begins with the majority patterns, the simplest, and works his way through the minority usages, the more difficult ones. There is also a good dictation drill for homonyms to distinguish the form which carries the written accent from the one which does not (*tú/tu, qué/que,* etc.).

This excellent article offers a sound linguistic account of the patterns which obtain for the use of the written accent in Spanish. It also provides some very usable examples of pattern drills designed to help solve the pedagogical problems the teacher and student must cope with in teaching and mastering the stress and accent features of Spanish.

85. SAVAIANO, EUGENE

"Does Teaching by the Audio-Lingual Approach Prepare the Student for Reading and Writing? ", *Hisp*, 43 (March, 1960), 62-66.

After pointing out that he taught Spanish using "new-key" techniques long before audiolingual procedures became popular, the author characterizes this approach in FL teaching and specifically turns his attention to the relationships between the oral and the written skills. He first considers reading, defined as sight-reading with comprehension, and maintains that only *good* (*sic*) students, after audiolingual contact with the language, actually manage any kind of smooth transition to the written word. This does not surprise Savaiano, however, for experience and observation have led him to the conclusion that many students manipulate oral drills and even "converse in fairly accurate and fluent Spanish" without knowing what they are saying. Therefore, that these students, often a sizeable segment of the class, cannot easily extract meaning from the written language is to be anticipated.

How can the teacher ascertain if the student, when first presented with reading material, is actually comprehending or merely reciting what he has drilled orally? The obvious answer is to rewrite the memorized material (dialogs, etc.), deviating markedly from the original, but including no new vocabulary or structures. Questionable is the author's suggestion that the teacher should read this "new" material aloud before assigning it as homework. Perhaps in the very early stages–but this is neither a testing nor a teaching procedure for reading, and certainly no means of finding out the student's ability to read Spanish.

An extended pre-reading period is suggested as a possible answer to the problem of overcoming the problematic transition from oral to written work.

Savaiano prefers instead his own modified version of "audio-lingual" teaching, one that calls for two or three fifty-minute class periods of exclusively oral practice (with books closed), employing the familiar audiolingual techniques. (It is regrettable that after more than ten years of considerable debate and some experimentation, and perhaps agreeing with the author, who is convinced that "regardless of the objective to be achieved from language study, even if its aim is to learn to read scientific materials, intensive practice in understanding and speaking . . . is still to be highly recommended as an aid in the development of accurate reading skills," we now possess only scanty evidence to support this belief.) After the third day, the students would first see the printed materials, and read them aloud for comprehension; the remaining work on the unit would be an alternation of oral and written practice. This sequence of changing emphases would, according to the author, allow the student to master each of the skills according to his own abilities.

Savaiano prefers this structure for each unit because it reduces the amount of segments intended for memorization alone (during that period of inevitable frustration for the eye-minded) and, also, because Spanish graphemes are not likely to produce interference. Interesting and arguable is the author's third reason; namely, that the students need some "visual crutch to support their efforts to retain what they hear." Many teachers will not agree, maintaining instead that the student must be made to rely on his ear in the process of learning to retain the spoken language, and to tolerate a certain level of frustration due to less than 100 percent comprehension.

While the author may "not see that requiring a student to read [cultural] materials for comprehension in the early stages in any way retards his ability to learn to pronounce or speak Spanish correctly," the point must be made that *no* amount of reading or writing can substitute for practice leading to mastery of the most difficult FL skill—speaking. Further, it is likely that practice in oral comprehension, not reading, facilitates more our ability to speak the FL.

Referring to reading more advanced materials, literature, the author comments on the efficacy of spending many hours looking up words, as if this trains us to retain lexical meaning merely because this tedious task is or comes to be hateful. The "no translation" rule is viewed as only encouraging half-understanding and sloppy reading habits.

Although this article provokes our reactions regarding the various considerations in learning to read and write in the FL, the author offers no concrete suggestions for techniques the teacher might adopt. And the problems of learning to write the FL are ignored altogether. The author seems to regard the ability to read and appreciate literature as the student's obvious goal. The typical FL student of the '70's will neither acknowledge nor accept this notion.

86. SEELYE, H. NED and J. LAURENCE DAY
      "Penetrating the Mass Media: A Unit to Develop Skill in Reading Spanish Newspaper Headlines," *FLA*, 5 (October, 1971), 69-81.

Since mass media are the source of much important news and topics of interest to students, the authors feel that magazines and newspapers can be effectively used in FL classrooms to stimulate interest in the language and especially the society it talks about. Moreover, our students are attuned to the media of their own culture, and it thus makes sense to assume that they can learn to enjoy and profit from FL radio broadcasts, films, magazines, newspapers, etc.

However, if newspapers, for example, are to become a usable source of this cultural insight and a springboard for conversation, the students must first be taught how to skim through the material. Otherwise, the student is likely to experience the typical reaction of being turned off by this exercise merely because he cannot get past the headlines. The point of the presentation is to help the student develop the needed skill. The article is a semiprogramed learning unit designed to teach the necessary specialized vocabulary and to develop in the learner the ability to spot stories relating to various topics.

The unit concentrates on three types of headlines: crime, social events, and sports. It is intended for students who are beyond the first semester of Spanish study. Terminal achievement is the student's ability to identify in twenty seconds and with 90 percent accuracy those headlines which announce these three topics. Ways to implement this learning unit: homework, peer-teaching, regular class activity. Time permitting, the suggestion is to spread newspaper reading throughout the term, if only for ten minutes a day.

Procedures: 1) Students become familiar with general newspaper format; 2) Study of Spanish topical word list, based on frequency and "clue" value, followed by recognition exercises requiring word identification in headlines; 3) Students check their ability to recognize the key words by underlining them in a group of typical headlines; 4) An exercise utilizing a vocabulary list, not entirely composed of clue words. The student is timed to develop speed in identifying only those words on the list which are key words. Students are asked to go through a list of twenty or so headlines and check only those which belong to the topic at hand. Speed is emphasized. Practice in identifying specific kinds of the general topics (sports, crime, social events, etc.) is helpful.

Since even native speakers often misread headlines from their own newspapers, most teachers are aware of the pitfalls awaiting their FL students when working through newspapers in the FL. Unfortunately, the authors fail to describe the causes of difficulties not lexical in nature: the special syntactic variations used in Spanish headlines, with ellipsis, inversion, etc., producing many kinds of ambiguities; and the orthographic obstacle created when upper-case letters are used.

87. TESCHNER, RICHARD VINCENT
    "The Written Accent in Spanish: A Programmed Lesson," *Hisp*, 54 (December, 1971), 885-894.

The problems involving use of the written accent in Spanish are all too neglected, according to Teschner, and as a consequence the student in the third-semester college course typically has not mastered the rules. Blame is placed with the textbook, which either ignores the topic or relegates it to footnote status. The author quite correctly points out that while rapid mastery of the Spanish graphemic system can be assured, the concepts needed to understand syllable division, diphthongization, phonemic stress, and so on are more "advanced" or sophisticated.

To teach correct use of the written accent in Spanish, Teschner has prepared a two-part lesson for intermediate students requiring two class periods. He relies heavily on minimal pairs to emphasize phonemic stress (*continuó - continuo*). Also treated is the role of the accent in breaking up diphthongs into two separate syllables. And the homographic monosyllables (*sé - se*). The author has chosen to syllabify all the examples himself, letting the student draw his own conclusions. The teacher can give more attention to syllabication if he wishes.

The lesson plan: Part I. A brief discussion of how the written accent mark is used in Spanish. Then: 1) words which end in consonants but which are not stressed on the last syllable; 2) words which end in vowels, but are not stressed on the next-to-last syllable; 3) examples of words with stress on other than the last or penult syllable; 4) the stress patterns—and required written mark—for words with two adjacent "weak" vowels, either as diphthongs or in hiatus; and 5) strong-weak and strong-strong combinations.

Part II. The written accent in 1) words of only one syllable; 2) direct and indirect questions; 3) exclamations; 4) demonstrative pronouns, 5) compound words; and 6) foreign words.

Exercises are provided for most of the sections, and at the end of the entire lesson there are fifty-four practice sentences.

For the most part the presentation is logical, clear and well synthesized, with good examples. The question for teachers is whether or not the problem of the written accent in Spanish warrants two days of study and practice. It would be interesting to have a large experimental group complete this lesson and compare its degree of mastery with that of a comparable group which would only be exposed to the usual textbook treatment.

VI. Drills and Drilling

88. FOSTER, DAVID WILLIAM
"A Model for Drilling Some Points of Grammar," *LL*, 15:1-2 (1965), 7-15.

Contrastive analysis reveals four different categories of native-target language relationships: 1) Points of overlap or convergence, with little or no interference, 2) Grammatical features which are non-existent in either the target or the source language, 3) Points of grammar which are both points of contact and points of divergence, where English has two or more ways or forms to handle what Spanish accomplishes with one (for example, Span. *su* vs. Engl. *his, her, its*), and 4) Like 3, but with the divergence in the target language (Engl. *you* vs. Span *tú* (or *vos*) and *Uds.*). Included in this last group of forever difficult learning problems are *por/para, ser/estar*, imperfect/preterite, and so on. That this category of troublemakers includes the most formidable obstacles for the learner is due to the fact that, unlike group 2, both semantic (or lexical) and syntactic distinctions are involved.

The main purpose of this article is to propose a model for drill sequences to teach such cases of semantic-syntactic split in Spanish. Foster insists that his own model conform in make-up to the standards generally maintained in good drills, but with the additional power to fix the distinctions which obtain in a pair like *Lo hago por ti* and *Lo hago para ti*. The author describes the methods used in certain textbooks to teach *por/para* and points out how each is ineffectual. The weakness in employing the translation technique (*Modern Spanish*) is that the two relator forms are not learned within the Spanish framework of referents. Attempts to account for the information graphically have other drawbacks, principally because many distinctions are not readily reducible to a set of pictures.

Foster would not exclude the approaches just mentioned, but he favors a model which can present the necessary distinctions within the target language. This is possible only to the extent the learner already commands the grammar with which to establish the contrasts. But very often such is the case. For example, the student can be made to see and can then learn the signal functions of *por* and *para* if the drill model utilizes sentences containing these prepositions in derived utterances:

Basic Sentence A:	A_1:	*Lo hace en mi lugar.*
	A_2:	*Lo hace por mí.*
Basic Sentence B:	B_1:	*Lo hace con el motivo de ayudarme.*
	B_2:	*Lo hace para mí.*

Unlike English "He does it for me," the derived Spanish sentences A_2 and

B$_2$ are unambiguous. And if in drilling the forms the student can keep in mind the basic differences as overtly seen in the basic sentences, he should, little by little, begin to internalize the function features for *por* and *para.* To acquire a total understanding and use of these he would perform a long series of transforms with *por*, then *para*, and finally with the two scrambled. The student is thus forced to make a choice based on information he has stored while remaining entirely in the target language. This kind of application of transformational devices has strong implications.

89. FREY, HERSCHEL J.
   "Audio-lingual Teaching and the Pattern Drill," *MLJ*, 52 (October, 1968), 349-355.

Before getting into a discussion of the nature of pattern drills and their function in teaching FL's (with particular emphasis on Spanish), the author first investigates the various methodological bases which incorporate at least some kind of drill exercises. Two principal FL learning theories are seen to co-exist: the habit formation theory and the rule generalization or "cognitive code-learning" theory. The former is characterized as generally consistent with audiolingual methods, while the grammar/rule approach is typically seen in a grammar-translation teaching situation. The author suggests, however, that regardless of what the individual teacher may think or say about his or her own teaching method and techniques, it is more often the case than not that no teacher consistently and without contradiction follows any particular "method" to the exclusion of all others, or at least with no elements from them. This is true mainly because many teachers have no clear theoretical understanding of method and, thus, do not and cannot be expected to put any well-formulated theory into practice.

   Since habit formation in FL acquisition implies the acquisition of competence through habit practice, the role that the pattern drill plays in the learning process is very important. Repetition which reveals analogy in language patterns and fixes sets of language information is the heart of pattern drill function. Further, such practice leads to automaticity, at least within the framework of the necessary stimulus-response situation. Implicit also in the audiolingual method is the understanding that while pattern drills per se do not qualify as true communication, the learner can, through appropriate guidance, transfer what he has "learned" to an actual situation demanding true language usage. Little empirical evidence is available in support of this transfer process or ability.

The author looks at what has been said regarding contrastive analysis and drills. Even when the drill segments incorporate considerable information from both languages, might it not be the case that the student is only working through surface features of the language and is not, in fact, generalizing about the FL in any meaningful way? But the author argues for more work in this area, the establishment of linguistic hierarchies, based on frequency and difficulty—this information to be incorporated into the drills.

Even the most cursory examination of language teaching materials reveals a heavy reliance on pattern drills as a primary means of teaching phonology, morphology and syntax. The term "pattern drill" has been misapplied, we are told, and is understood to include only those drills which in their execution focus the learner's attention on one change at a time when this change occurs consistently within the same phonological or grammatical frame.

An adequate classification of all pattern drills includes only four main types: 1) the repetition drill; 2) the substitution drill; 3) the transformation or construction drill; and 4) the translation drill. While it is clear that many users and producers of pattern drills are unaware of the exact functions of each type, certain patterns (of expectations) can be identified. The repetition drill has been considered effective in drilling phonology and, to an extent, vocabulary, but its form suggests limited application to grammar. The item substitution drill has been judged quite productive in teaching a language's arbitrary system of matching and agreement—especially for Spanish which, unlike English, requires considerable overt concordance. Even irregular forms can be attacked through this pattern drill. The transformation (or construction) pattern drill is easily the least understood of the four types. Often involving a permutation which results in some similar version of the original drill sentence, this drill process may, in some applications, reveal pertinent interrelationships between constructs, thereby creating in the learner an intuition for awareness of some features of the new language. Translation drills are seen as the most useful in testing or teaching those knotty problem areas of the target language which deviate in complicated ways from the native tongue. The author points out that many textbooks "resort" to translation drills when good pattern drills kept in the FL are hard to come by.

Other considerations: The most appropriate sequence of drill and grammatical discussion. Shortcomings of the pattern drill. Drilling and class pace. Drill content. Drills vs. actual speech. Personalizing drills. Speculation as to the future of pattern drills.

90. GAARDER, A. BRUCE
       "Beyond Grammar and Beyond Drills," *FLA*, 1 (December, 1967), 109-118.

Presents a teaching strategy to guide the student beyond structural pattern drills to spontaneous, liberated expression. The suggestion is to exploit the automaticity that comes with over-learning. Instead of conceding that the student's ability to memorize and learn via analogy function is ordinarily exhausted through drilling and the other audiolingual practices, Gaarder argues that more can be expected of the student. He claims that by applying the "principle of control" (control by the language, but especially control of the language) to assure language practice as life experience, with logical situational reality, the learner can take full advantages of his abilities. The author would not have the beginning student restricted very long to rote learning; instead he should be allowed to recombine without a model what he has learned through memorized dialogs and pattern drills.

Rather than being concerned as to when and whether the student has induced a rule and therefore understands and can use a structure, Gaarder puts more emphasis on the student's "having generated every possible utterance regarding each basic dialog-narrative that can be made within the limits of his total life experience in the language up to that point in time." To achieve this functional control, the student must perform drills that concentrate on significant meaning as well as structure. Each drill should be "a conversation with you, the learner." The author allows that drills may include multiple structural features, though only one should be new, and therefore stressed. This personalization of the sentence implies that attention is drawn away from the grammar per se.

Gaarder shows what conversational, mainly recombination-type drills are like. The situational context of each drill is kept as close as possible to that of the dialog. The point to be noted for these drills is that, unlike the great majority, they focus the learner's attention on the "*event*" *and* on the new structure. In other words, drills become language as communication, since the student becomes personally and meaningfully involved.

A part of the author's suggested procedure is "contrastive meaning analysis," through which the student understands and says everything possible up to each point. Nothing can be left to chance, we are told, though the teacher need not be conscious of all that is going on, since "by isolating and focusing the student's attention successively on every possible relationship, every fact, implication, and assumption in relation to all others, all of the grammar relationships are necessarily covered." This is probably true, though not demonstrably so.

The first of several sample analyses for a general outline appears too difficult and involved for the student "somewhere in the first semester." Gaarder's method will run this risk, but in general longer utterances and considerable complexity are possible when drill sentences are personalized.

The author ends his engaging article by outlining the necessary teacher competence for this kind of inductive learning. The less able teacher could utilize the strategy, with guidance, as well as the master teacher, who requires more flexibility. Individualized, programed learning could incorporate the entire analysis and drill types suggested here. A variety of sample drill types is appended.

91. GOLINKIN, BLOSSOM D.

"Some Pedagogic Tools for Third-Year College Spanish Classes," *Hisp*, 54 (September, 1971), 493-495.

Discusses three questions of approach or technique: 1) how to work with idioms based on literary readings; 2) the use of the question-answer technique for literature; and 3) the choice of reading matter for the third-year college class, i.e., selections vs. whole works.

This teacher stresses the importance of teaching idioms, particularly at the more advanced level. Mere passive control of these expressions is not enough. It is suggested that the student compile his own list of idiomatic expressions, taken from what he reads, so that he becomes "idiom conscious." One way of having the student achieve an active command of idioms is to expect him to come to class prepared to use the expressions in original sentences. The teacher in turn can prepare his own list of useful idioms. Procedure for practice: a student copies the teacher's list on the board, students are asked to write original sentences incorporating these idioms, and after working with the literary text from which the idioms have been extracted, time out is taken to concentrate on sentence building (both orally and in written form). The point is that the study of idioms can have a place in the study of literature.

The inventing of questions based on literature: The author suggests that the students work up a series of questions with answers for literary selections which have no accompanying exercises. With the students directing the questions and answers, the teacher does not monopolize speaking time and the class can profit from both more practice time and the responsibility. This responsibility can be shared by each member of the class if the questions are corrected by the students as they are asked. The real dangers in this approach include of course an imperfect and less than highly productive model and a likely slowdown in pace. On the other hand, what the student loses in economy is perhaps made up for by the additional practice (especially in creating new sentences of his own).

Concerning the familiar polemic over literary selections vs. whole works, Golinkin favors careful choice of incomplete excerpts. She bases her argument on course goals and believes that since the third year student is experiencing his final exposure to the FL and its literature, the reading of entire works uses up too much class time and precludes the desirable sampling of a variety of forms and authors. Not without merit is the author's insistence that first the student's interest must be aroused by reading some of the highlights of Spanish literature, if he is to proceed on his own. The problems involved in selection of material are not discussed.

92. HADLICH, ROGER L.
    "Lexical Contrastive Analysis," *MLJ*, 49 (November, 1965),
    426-429.

Acknowledging the pedagogical theory which maintains that FL students have the most difficulty learning those target-language elements which differ most from their native language, Hadlich suggests that, contrary to traditional approach, the lexical problems created by pairing can best be solved not by utilization of contrastive grammar, but instead by some alternative procedures. The author first cites the familiar phonological and morphosyntactic pairs which cause trouble in learning Spanish (English /s/ and /z/; Spanish *salir/dejar, por/para,* etc.) and allows that teaching experience and tradition support contrastive analysis in approaching these problem areas.

But, based on results obtained in an experimental study at the University of Michigan, Hadlich concludes that, paradoxically, lexical "problem pairs" were found to be less difficult for those students who were forced to avoid the customary comparisons. Thus, pairs such as *conocer/saber, ser/estar,* etc. were not presented to the students either together or as problem words. Each of these lexical items appeared singly. The result was that the students controlled these pairs markedly better than the other first-year Spanish students who had worked through them in the conventional fashion. They were even surprised to learn later, in translating sentences, that such pairs existed and that two different words in Spanish were represented by only one in English.

These findings are presented as a challenge to the assumption that control of these lexical pairs is best achieved through contrastive presentation. The question is then asked: Should they instead be taught as if no problem existed, that the application of contrastive procedures in this lexical area is misleading, even harmful? "Yes" is Hadlich's answer.

The assumption is that a pair such as *dejar* and *salir*, for example, are essentially unrelated by the native speaker and therefore in their linguistic identity (as are English *make* and *do*). Hadlich's point, then, is that "problem pairs" are nonnative, that the relation between the two members is extraneous to the target language and any attempt to view them otherwise is incorrect and pedagogically unsound.

The author also challenges the method of teaching these problem-pair distinctions. Translation should not, he thinks, be used to focus the learner's attention on the English "equivalents," since this forces the student to use native language criteria for understanding second language distinctions. And even those drills which do not include translation produce unnecessary confusion by effecting an invalid pairing: "*Salí de casa pero dejé el sombrero.*" Hadlich believes that this type of drill will only encourage erroneous substitution, evidencing contrastive analysis as a "self-fulfilling prophesy."

Though proof of the negative effects are not to be found in the author's relatively small student sample, the theoretical assumption certainly warrants further investigation. Hadlich is quite correct in pointing out that, after all, words must be learned within the grammatical and contextual restrictions of the target language, that any contrastive information must be either unlearned or ignored in actual communication. When pattern overlap does occur (*saber/conocer* + *que*; *dejar/salir* + place, etc.) within the structural range of a given pair, it is of low frequency and an exception to general usage and should be omitted from the early stages of language study. But only controlled teaching and testing of these lexical items among large student groups could determine the extent of confusion by learners who study and practice the contrasts, or the avoidance of such confusion by learners who ignore the traditional word pairs.

93. O'CONNOR, PATRICIA
   "A Film Strip for Pattern Drill," *LL*, 5:1-2 (1953-54), 43-47.

Film strips were used at the University of Texas for pattern drilling of certain special problems which arise after the student has acquired some familiarity with the FL. If recourse to English and the written word are to be avoided—the learner is still at the pre-spelling stage—the teacher is limited as to the techniques available to assure progress. Mere repetition, though necessary, is not enough, because it lulls the student with its boring monotony.

The film strip was found to be very effective in adding the needed variety. Each consists of thirty-six frames illustrating twenty basic item-substitution pattern drills. (The sample pattern drill is actually of the combined-pattern-replacement variety, and it is not clear that all are not the same.) The content of these films is kept as simple as possible; stick figures people the frames.

The drills fulfill two functions in that they provide practice in both pronunciation and structure. The sentences were selected from a series of pronunciation exercises containing specific problems. The students liked the film strips because they had the sense of "talking about something" from the earliest stages of their contact with Spanish. New words were presented via the films and by the time the basic textbook was introduced (after four or five weeks), the students had already attained a grasp of the simplest structures—not to mention a good command of the phonology.

These film strips proved useful as in-class stimulation for conversation and for testing. The author never states in so many words, though the implication is here, that this kind of visual aid allows a bypass of specious word cues and, to an extent, of oral stimulus, and is the closest thing to a non-cue available for classroom (or lab) practice.

VII. Methodology and Method Evaluation

94. BLICKENSTAFF, CHANNING B. and FRANK J. WOERDEHOFF
"A Comparison of the Monostructural and Dialogue Approaches
to the Teaching of College Spanish," *MLJ*, 51 (January, 1967),
14-23.

Presents the results of a study comparing the effectiveness of the
monostructural and dialogue approaches to the teaching of audiolingual
college Spanish. The data were taken from the posttested group of 72
students at Purdue University, randomly divided into the two
experimental groups. Each group was comprised of two sections averaging
20-25 students each. The results were obtained after two semesters of
Spanish study.

A careful and detailed listing is made of the kinds of activities that took
place in the classes. These conform to the generally accepted definition of
audiolingual teaching. *A Structural Course in Spanish*, by D. L. Wolf, R. L.
Hadlich, and J. G. Inman was the text chosen for the monostructural
sections and J. A. Thompson and A. Berumen's *Speaking and
Understanding Spanish*, for the dialog group. S. H. Wofsy's *Lecturas
Fáciles y Útiles* was used as a supplementary reader for both groups. The
authors felt that some of the differences pointed up in the posttests were
attributable to the fact that only in the dialog group was the reader used at
regular intervals, with a too late and too concentrated use by the
non-dialog group. Though one can question the choice of the
Thompson-Berumen text as a "typical" dialog text, the authors no doubt
preferred it to others because of its vocabulary and drill content which
closely parallels that of the monostructural text.

Although the participating teachers and students represent too small an
experimental group to afford convincing results, the design and control of
the study are commendable. Even after the inevitable attrition, the
posttested groups show remarkable similarities as to sex, age, class,
interests, background, and the like. The students were presumably
unaware of being involved in an experiment (and thus, not vulnerable to
the Hawthorne effect), while the instructors made every effort to bring
equal skill, technique and commitment to the two groups. Indeed, the
teachers were judged of quite equal competence and appeal on a
fifteen-item attitude inventory poll.

Ten posttests were administered to the students in each approach
group. The reliability factor was high for all except the speaking test (with
a coefficient of .86). Findings: As subjected to a multiple analysis of
covariance and adjusted for initial differences on the pretests, the data
revealed a higher degree of achievement by the dialog group on every test,
except the MLA Speaking Test and the Change in Interest Test (slight
difference for both). This overall superiority of the dialog students was

more pronounced for the writing, reading, vocabulary, and grammar tests than for listening and comprehension. This variance could be explained either as the result of teacher or material difference, or both.

The authors were unable to satisfactorily explain why twice as many of the monostructural students indicated they intended to pursue additional Spanish courses. Perhaps this as much as anything led the participating teachers and the authors to conclude that their results indicate justification of further investigation of the monostructural concept.

95. CHASTAIN, KENNETH D. and FRANK J. WOERDEHOFF
    "A Methodological Study Comparing the Audio-Lingual Habit Theory and the Cognitive Code-Learning Theory," *MLJ*, 52 (May, 1968), 268-279.

The purpose of this interesting study is to report the results of an experimental project involving two different approaches to teaching Spanish. The data were collected in 1965 at Purdue University and represented some six sections—169 students; 82 in an "audio-lingual" group and 87 in a "cognitive code-learning" group. Although the authors are careful to define and characterize each method, unless they have omitted certain details the two groups shared several important instructional features and it is not surprising that the two posttested groups demonstrated about equal performance in the four skills after a year's FL study.

Whereas the audiolingual group memorized dialogs, did pattern drills and learned grammar inductively, the cognitive group (not to be confused with the traditional "grammar-translation" method) was exposed to deductive explanation of grammar prior to any practice. However, all the students involved in this experiment seem to have performed many of the same things. Both groups practiced the material in some kind(s) of drills or exercises (including heavy use of the question-answer technique), and also made use of the language laboratory—though the audiolingual students probably attended more regularly. No teachers did translations and a great deal of oral work was done in the code-learning classes. And the code-learning students appear to have benefited from considerably more contextual practice. In fact, the audiolingual group was apparently deprived of any personalized or liberated expression. The authors seem to have insisted that the audiolingual teachers stick to mechanical drills or, at best, questions based on the dialogs.

The implications of the conclusions are weakened by the fact that the classes averaged more than twenty-seven students per section. Even if this balance means one more controlled variable among the experimental groups, one must understand that of necessity audiolingual teaching requires considerable individual recitation. This is not to imply that a code-learning group would not also greatly benefit from more individual work, but it is very likely the case that of the two, the audiolingual group will suffer more if individual practice is limited.

One can seriously question the choice of *Cuentos y risas* as the second semester reader used by all students to accompany *Modern Spanish* (the two audiolingual classes) and *Beginning Spanish, A Cultural Approach* (the other two). Only careful study would reveal the advantage that one group might have over the other, and one guess would be that the audiolingual group, using the MLA text which stresses structure, would experience the greater amount of linguistic shock in transferring from one text to the other, producing a loss of learning yield which would last throughout the second semester.

Exact findings: a slight but general superiority of the code-learning students. The cognitive group could understand and speak Spanish at least as well as the audiolingual group and their scores on the written tests were better. The only difference singled out in favor of the audiolingual students was their imitative ability. Although the tests given to both groups permitted objective evaluation, and every effort was made to assure objectivity, the speaking tests were scored by two native speakers who, although working independently, had a reliability coefficient of only .72.

The conclusions drawn from this experiment must be carefully studied. For although the variables were for the most part quite controlled and favored neither group, only four teachers and ninety-nine posttested students were involved in the study—too few for any "meaningful" conclusions. Obviously the superiority of only one teacher (and with one less than inspiring instructor in the opposite group) would significantly invalidate comparative results. It is regrettable that prevailing teaching situations have precluded studies involving very large controlled groups, but this is the only kind of experiment which will ultimately allow us to state as fact that, for example, analysis is superior to analogy, that deductive presentation is more productive than inductive, that an all-senses approach is superior to the natural order of presentation, and so on.

96. GUERRA, MANUEL H.
   "Is Conversation Enough? A Reappraisal of Beginning Foreign Language Instruction," *Hisp*, 43 (May, 1960), 249-252.

Questions the advisability of an exclusively aural-oral approach for the FLES program. Though acknowledging the advantages of a FL program based on the primacy of speech over writing, Guerra sees audiolingual teaching as "wonderful—but only up to a point." This point is that inevitable moment when boredom sets in because the student has been saturated with hearing and imitating and deprived of visual stimulation.

When does this day arrive, and what can be done about the problem? The author, writing only a few years after Sputnik and the ensuing almost unanimous acceptance of an all-oral approach to FL in the grades, voices one of the first thoughtful doubts about the efficacy of a protracted period without some reading in the FL. Noting that FLES advocates had begun to revise some of their original thinking, Guerra perceives a reappraisal triggered by negative experience. But while "adaptability" should be an important consideration for any intelligent stance, his strongest argument for reinstating the book in the classroom is *not* that "most teachers are book-oriented" and cannot be realistically expected to function successfully surrounded by audio materials. Rather, Guerra is talking against a two- or three-year program devoid of written Spanish. Under such circumstances, to delimit the possibilities for variety is indeed unwise, and the author's concept of language learning as the natural process being the whole process, i.e., involving all skills, makes sense. Imaginative books containing colorful, engaging pictures help the student fix the language information. The teacher can take the necessary steps to make sure that visual materials do not displace emphasis on comprehension and speaking. This is not always easy, however, and several precautions must be taken lest the classroom activities gravitate too much in any direction. When the teacher senses that the students feel too insecure and their expressed preferences betray either inadequate command of what has been studied or too heavy a reliance on the book, then review work and expanded practice is in order.

The time to introduce the written language for reading is after the student has become "thoroughly accustomed to hearing, understanding and speaking simple sentences, using a basic vocabulary." After this point the textbook materials can be utilized in a multiplicity of ways: word repetition, dramatization, guessing games, suggestion, checkup, etc.

97. MAYNES, J. OSCAR, Jr.
        "An Experiment to Gauge the Effectiveness of the Audio-lingual
        Method and the Language Lab," *Hisp*, 45 (May, 1962), 377-382.

Presents the results of a small-scale experiment with a two-fold purpose: 1) measure the effectiveness of the audiolingual method, and 2) justify the use of the language laboratory. Maynes and the cooperating teachers judged the experiment to be successful on both counts.

Two groups of high-school students (a control class and an experimental class) studied elementary Spanish for eighteen weeks. Whereas the experimental group worked with dialogs containing grammar taught via pattern drills (and with overlearning in the lab), the control group, though working with the same materials, stressed grammar, then reading, writing, speaking and understanding, in this order. The objective of the experimental class was to emphasize understanding and speaking; reading and writing were in the main based on the already mastered oral material.

Tests were given in five areas: oral question and answer, oral comprehension, reading comprehension, grammar, and culture. The author does not specify the test formats. Results of these tests showed superiority of the experimental group for all skills, especially the speaking skill. The participating teacher and the evaluators noticed that as the year progressed the control class became more passive, while oral participation in the other group apparently generated enthusiasm even in the slow students. There were five native speakers in each class, but only in the experimental group did these students inspire the nonnatives to interact with them and use their native speech as a model.

The evaluators felt that the particular method used to present the grammar to the experimental students accounted for their demonstrated superiority on the oral comprehension and the question-answer response tests. Further, they considered vital the role that the language lab played in giving a decided advantage to the more successful group.

Though Maynes and his helpers who participated in this experiment saw to it that the two groups were balanced as to student makeup, including I.Q., GPA, grade level, sex, and native knowledge of Spanish, other important variables are not accounted for. These would include the teacher, the nature of the tests, student FL aptitude, and so on. And the fact that only two classes provided data for the experiment weakens any conclusions one might wish to draw from the test results.

98. RICHARDS, S. EARLE and JOAN E. APPEL
    "The Effects of Written Words in Beginning Spanish," *MLJ*, 40 (March, 1956), 129-133.

An experiment to determine the effects of using written words in teaching elementary Spanish. The authors also hoped to discover relationships between the results of linguistic aptitude pretests and achievement posttests.

Twenty-eight college juniors and seniors at Boston University were divided into two groups (control and experimental) matched for I.Q., sex, age, class, and years of FL study. One instructor taught all students using an "audio-visual direct method"—the only difference being that the experimental section saw no written words. Spanish was studied for three weeks.

The series of pretests, taken from John B. Carroll's *A Factor Analysis of Verbal Abilities*, included a test for paired associates, memory for homophone word squares, auditory memory span for related and unrelated words, disarranged morphemes, and speed of articulation. The three posttests covered Spanish vocabulary, aural comprehension, (both with a multiple-choice picture format), and oral fluency and pronunciation. The latter was found to be the easiest to devise but the most difficult to administer and score. The testees were asked to produce on tape one complete Spanish sentence for each of twelve sequent pictures.

Results: Differences between the pretest scores were not significant enough to establish correlations with the achievement tests. Predictably, the experimental group tested higher in oral reproduction and pronunciation, but only slightly better in aural comprehension and vocabulary. The authors felt that the more successful group profited from the experimental treatment involving interaction of the oral skills, and with no interference from the written word.

Larger groups and longer instruction periods would be needed to corroborate these findings and provide answers for some of the questions brought out in this experiment.

99. SACKS, NORMAN P.
"*Modern Spanish* in an Intensive Program for Graduate Students: An Experiment and Some Reflections," *Hisp*, 50 (May, 1967), 310-319.

The results of an intensive experimental class of graduate students (social science majors) at the University of Wisconsin, 1965. Apart from providing needed instruction in elementary Spanish to these students, the purpose of the project was to find out how students with no prior study of Spanish would compare with others who had studied the language and to see how advanced students would react to audio-visual aids (the films and *Visual Grammar Posters* for *Modern Spanish*, the text used in the course).

The participating students represented a homogeneous and highly motivated group. The course was taught by three instructors following a tight, carefully planned schedule.

"Lessons" gleaned from this experiment: 1) Variety of class content is essential, but adequate time must be spent in learning each structure and each skill; 2) all procedures and reasons behind the general *modus operandi* must be clearly understood; 3) the students exhibited the usual obstacles in learning audiolingually (reluctance to depend on the ear, or to memorize dialogs, interference from English, inability to keep up with a fast pace, etc.); 4) interference from classroom conditioning, in particular passivism; 5) an intensive class schedule limits time for digestion; 6) considerable time was required for mastery of each dialog. Few students could supply the corresponding dialog sentences for the filmed dialogs with the sound track off; 7) the most tiring pattern drills should be relegated to the language lab; 8) good results were obtained from prepared questions based on the dialogs and reworked readings, some on cultural topics.

A post-course questionnaire was prepared to ascertain student reactions to the various learning aids, the difficulties in adjusting to audiolingual procedures, the importance of previous study of Spanish, the class schedule, translations, the transition from oral to written work, etc. The specific comments repeat those obtained from other audiolingual experiments.

General conclusions: Mature students seem to react favorably to audiovisual aids. They also feel the need for "grammar," with emphasis on contrastive explanations. Reworking of familiar material is necessary for continued motivation. Some confusion by students as to what actual conversation is. Questionnaires are tricky and students are not always in a position to know what they have learned or how. Students are impressed with careful organization. Intellectual and cultural content of materials is essential even in an introductory course.

VIII. Material Evaluation

100. CHASTAIN, KENNETH
"Selecting a Basic Text: A Subjective Evaluation," *Hisp*, 54 (September, 1971), 483-487.

In order to avoid missing the forest because of the trees, and preferring not to base textbook evaluation on any available lists of objective criteria, Chastain proposes simply a subjective approach. He believes that this is the better way to make a selection based on the crucial compatibility between materials and the teaching practices of the teacher. If the author is correct in believing teaching to be a subjective interpretation of textual materials, then a "personal" appraisal would seem advisable. Another reason to reject the suggested objective criteria, according to the author, is that they are built around preferences—usually audiolingual—as to method, and since no method can claim solid theoretical support, a teacher's decision should be based on what seems logical to him.

Chastain establishes these assumptions on which to base his criteria for material evaluation:

1. A student learns what he actually does in the FL;
2. A student should be made to feel successful;
3. The classroom needs much variety;
4. The student must understand, practice (drill), and expand his acquired skills;
5. The teacher should not expect too much—usually no more than for the student to approach mastery of the FL;
6. All four language skills should be practiced;
7. The FL should be related to the people who natively speak it;
8. Homework assignments should be practical and specific— necessary for successful classroom performance.

Criteria for selecting a text (as based on the foregoing assumptions):

1. Since self-expression in the FL is essential, even beginning with the student's first attempts, vocabulary and content of the dialogs (or reading materials) should facilitate "liberated expression." The student has to be able to use the vocabulary to talk about his own life.

2. Emphasis should allow performance of the three steps in language acquisition: understanding, practice, and free expression. The student is to be guided with a minimum of error, a maximum of confidence.

3. Practice of all four skills plus some culture. There is perhaps considerably less transfer from one language skill to another than has been thought. Culture should be presented simply and in the FL.

4. A proper progression of difficulty in developing the language skills. This is, of course, easier sought than found. Not only do we know very little about the interrelationships of the four FL skills, but about language hierarchy (meaning both structure and difficulty levels) as well.

5. Homework assignments should be definite, non-frustrating, and intended as class preparation (performance), mastery by the students to be rewarded.

In advocating this less than scientific *modus operandi* for textbook selection, the author seems especially concerned about avoiding a bad "fit" between materials and teacher. There is some danger, however, in advising some teachers to base their decisions on their (current) teaching techniques and past experience. Many teachers have been willing and even eager (though not always so able) to ignore both in seeking materials which might add new and successful approaches to their task.

101. MOYE DEL BARRIO, MARGARET
"Emergence of a Spanish Television Course for FLES," *MLJ*, 49 (April, 1965), 212-216.

A reassessment of the effectiveness of a FLES program televised in certain Detroit classrooms. Concern arose after oral tests produced disappointing results. It was found that the students became noun-oriented rather than speech-oriented, that while they could, for example, respond to and produce topical material, memorized utterances, etc., they could not in effect speak Spanish. The teachers involved in this program concluded that the course should be structure-centered and emphasize speech as real communication. The question was how to maneuver the pupils from stimulus-guided to free responses. The answer was found in dialogs.

The dialogs which developed as a result of the unsuccessful period ending in 1961 were to be linguistically valid and at the same time interesting and functional for the young learners. The writers strove for natural, live talk. Instead of deliberately building sentences ("artificial talk") around grammar items or specific noun categories, they caught spontaneous language on the fly and used those phrases which contained the necessary grammar and vocabulary. Some lexical items were changed and most of the dialog sentences were reused as pattern practice drills.

Using the *Simón dice* teaching technique, the author compares the typically artificial sequence with a more natural one to teach the parts of the body and the days of the week. Too many of the contrived dialogs, Moye del Barrio correctly points out, are anything but true-to-life simply because they focus on lexical sets and ironically prove uneconomical in the end.

Other characteristics found to be essential to these *escenitas* at their best were 1) personal involvement of the child, 2) short dialogs with short lines, 3) colloquial speech patterns, 4) avoidance of lists of vocabulary items, 5) words and sentences in context, and 6) interjections and transitional words. In addition, the usability of the dialogs was judged according to their building power for follow-up activities, including pattern practice, games, songs, etc.

Although this article does not take up the matter of technique, especially as to its adaptation in televised teaching, it does clearly outline the requirements for productive dialogs.

102. SACKS, NORMAN P.
      "The Art of the Spanish Textbook, 1917-1967," *Hisp*, 50 (December, 1967), 875-887.

A comprehensive survey covering fifty years of development in Spanish textbooks, including grammars, edited literary selections, and other materials for the classroom. The dramatic developments in the field of linguistics are cited as the reason for the great variety in these materials and the subsequent and not infrequent confusion on the part of the users.

In examining the ever-increasing proliferation of textbooks, Sacks appropriately asks (or, rather, asks of the authors) several necessary questions. What is the intended audience for the new book? What real needs will it fill? Will the textbook be a significant contribution? Before the would-be author sits down to his writing task (or labor of love), Sacks would have him consider three basic criteria: 1) scholarly accuracy and up-to-dateness of the material; 2) pedagogical harmony of content and objectives; 3) relevance to the intended users.

The author acknowledges the great demands high standards of writing make upon an author, but still insists that he do all the composition, down to the last drill. He must know what to include and what to omit and, more importantly, clearly conceptualize his project. A first-rate grammar requires as its author a master teacher and a solid linguist, one who knows both native and target languages extremely well. In addition to these qualifications, the author needs a firm control of cultural information and, in the case of edited literary materials, an appreciation of the spirit and content of what he chooses. He will also have to make good judgements when the inevitable clash of loyalties arises, between the original (modified) text, the student's needs, the publisher's requests or demands, and the author's own integrity.

Sacks examines the various problems involved in producing successful editions and names many of the prose, poetic and dramatic works studied by generations of Spanish students. Until the forties teachers appeared to be content to stress early literature. Siglo de Oro plays, for example, abounded. The short story was also widely used. In general the novel did not fare so well, as editors abridged at will and badly. And the author is correct in noting that, especially as regards the novel, students were not reading the best Hispanic literature. Poetry has consistently come in a distant third, and Latin American literature is only now receiving its due. Since about 1930, more effort has been made to publish texts outside the conventional molds, and the essay in particular has risen in popularity.

Reviewing the old and the new, Sacks maintains commendable objectivity and misses very few grammars and edited texts. It would be difficult to overemphasize the importance of the textbook in determining the content and the quality of a Spanish class. While the author points to no perfect textbook, he believes that the general level of excellence has risen considerably, since the printed material our students use these days is more interesting, varied, sophisticated and sound than that of fifty or even ten years ago.

103. SHEPPARD, DOUGLAS C.
"What Text Shall I Use?", *Hisp*, 43 (December, 1960), 565-567.

An extract of a lecture given by the author to a course in language analysis in an NDEA FL Institute.

A good textbook would:

1) not insist on written exercises until the student has done considerable oral work;

2) contain comparisons between the sound systems of English and Spanish, with accurate illustrations and examples;

3) begin the description and practice of intonation early and continue it throughout the text;

4) present one valid dialect of Spanish and a language not beyond the reach of the student (i.e., avoid introduction to "literary masterpieces");

5) introduce vocabulary only in meaningful contexts;

6) not attempt to be everything to everybody;

7) be based on principles of linguistics; and

8) call for little, if any, translation.

The author concludes that to insist on all the above criteria in selecting a textbook, at least seventy-five percent of the then currently available materials would have to be rejected. Sheppard correctly predicted a change in the nature of teaching materials, anticipating the appearance of more and more audiolingual textbooks. Editing inferior materials is given as one solution to a (hopefully) temporary problem.

The reader will note the absence among the above list of several important earmarks of superior teaching materials.

104. SICILIANO, ERNEST A.
"Common Sense in Our Texts," *Hisp*, 47 (May, 1964), 350-354.

The interest in this article is its calling into question the quality and format of materials that are advertised as "audiolingual." The author has these basic criticisms: 1) (Dialog) sentences for beginning FL instruction should not be taped at normal speed; 2) Students should not be expected to comprehend new combinations of previously learned language segments; 3) Publishers should not retread old texts, albeit with accompanying tapes, and proffer them as audiolingual; 4) No one text should attempt to present all four skills; 5) An introductory conversational grammar should contain valid everyday topics, minimum vocabulary for each unit, and only essential and clear grammar rules. While points 3 and 5 are reasonable, the others are untenable.

Though Siciliano judges all available texts to fall short of his ideal, he singles out *Modern Spanish* (Harcourt-Brace, 1960) as equally unworthy of his use (presumably all the more so because its authors *should* have known better). Some of his criticisms are indeed valid, and have been voiced by many if not most of the teachers who have used this cornerstone textbook. For example, the needlessly long sentences for repetition, the length (450 pp.) of the text, the convergence of too many points of grammar in one unit, and the like. Less convincing is his denouncement of some of the drill types and the problems posed by Unit I (pronunciation) for the "solid" teacher unfamiliar with linguistic terminology. The author insists that this first unit cannot be covered in one week; but many teachers do it—well and enjoyably. And if the book's exercises on Spanish intonation "will be entirely and irrevocably disregarded, ... [and will] confound the student," then it is likely that either the teacher is not competent or else does not include among his goals the acquisition of acceptable patterns of pronunciation by the student.

The real value of this article is that it asks some of the right questions and demonstrates that ignorance is not always bliss. Lamentably, many of the more interesting and important features of *Modern Spanish* which have been profitably discussed by dedicated, serious, troubled, disappointed and informed teachers of Spanish are not brought out by Siciliano, whose "unprofessionally humble opinion" is that *Modern Spanish* poses more problems than it solves.

IX. The Language
Laboratory

105. BARRUTIA, RICHARD

"The Language Laboratory," in *A Handbook for Teachers of Spanish and Portuguese*, edited by Donald D. Walsh. Lexington, Mass.: D. C. Heath and Co., 1969, 79-88.

An excellent and uncomplicated synthesis of the function and use of the language laboratory. Pointing out that much time and energy have been misspent in uncovering facts about the language lab which have no productive application in FL teaching, Barrutia discusses under three topics the basic knowledge which *does* determine a successful language laboratory operation:

1) What is a language lab? The user—both the teacher and student—should know what the laboratory can do, what it is for, and what are its limitations. "The lab is no more than a place where certain kinds of recorder-assisted learning (RAL) can take place." It is not a teaching machine, which fact has surprised and disappointed those who have erroneously assigned to it tasks it could never perform. Nor should the lab ever have been intended to reduce the teacher's work; it can only increase it, rearrange it, redirect it, and (hopefully) make it more effective. The teaching objectives should determine the nature of the lab. The less expensive and complicated electronic classroom might better serve the needs of high school students, who cannot always profit maximally from the compare-and-evaluate procedure.

2) How does it work? The taped program is dependent on stimulus-response learning, which includes the acquisition of automatic habits and the development of skills. Pronunciation, intonation, comprehension, practice with oral cues—these are areas in which the lab can supplement the class and the textbook. Other arguments for the lab are that it can model consistently, give the fatigued teacher a respite, and test the student. Barrutia chooses not to discuss the possible use of visuals in the lab, especially in the advanced stages when they could serve as complex non-graphic stimuli.

3) How do teachers interact with the laboratory and the students in order to maximize learning? Ironically Barrutia judges the human being to be the most important part of the machinery. No lab program will be truly successful unless the teacher who coordinates its use stays abreast of new developments and involves himself directly in improving what he has. When possible, the teacher's own voice should be taped. The author outlines a new format for dialog presentation [See No. 108 for a fuller treatment by Barrutia].

Appended is Donald D. Walsh's list of twelve "Do's and Don'ts for Planning and Operating a Language Lab or an Electronic Classroom in a High School" (New York: MLA, 1961).

106. GARNETT, NORMA A.
"Making the Language Laboratory Effective," *Hisp*, 50 (May, 1967), 319-322.

The author dismisses the "to be or not to be" issue surrounding the language laboratory as outdated. The only question, as Garnett sees the matter, is how best to utilize the facility. She shares her experiences, her successful procedures as well as experiments, in this convincing report of what the teacher and the student can do with the lab at the high school level.

The essentials: 1) regularly scheduled, short lab sessions; 2) correlated tapes of dialogs, drills, listening comprehension material, and review work; 3) laboratory work should be graded, giving that much more status to its integral part in the total program; 4) extra experimental tapes, combining oral and written work, slides, culture and dictation (the students meet these fresh, as they are unannounced)—most anything to effect added motivation and demonstrable learning.

The desirability of demonstrating to the student his improvement via the lab cannot be overstated. And teachers should realize that they have by no means explored the possibilities for making of the language laboratory a true teaching machine. The best prospects would seem to lie in imaginative materials which do not repeat the text or homework. The use of visual stimuli for drills and conversation is also a possibility worth more investigation.

107. PHILLIPS, ROBERT
"Using the Tape Recorder to Correct Student Compositions," *Hisp*, 51 (March, 1968), 126-127.

A method for correcting advanced compositions which the author has used to overcome various problems. Phillips had discouragingly experienced student apathy toward his carefully written corrections. The grade, not the FL mistakes, seemed to make the only impression. Another problem was that this teacher felt unable to write out the corrections in such a way that the student knew what and why he was composing incorrectly.

Since class time cannot be used to go over each error in every student's composition, the language laboratory provides the answer. Phillips experienced good results in taping his corrections to students' papers, which the individual student later read against the teacher's taped comments. Short comments can be made for minor mistakes, but for more serious ones an identifying number can be marked in the text. Then after the whole paper has been reviewed, the teacher can return to these numbers and give full corrections and suggestions for each. This procedure takes little more time, if any, than the conventional method of marking compositions.

A second method, preferred by the author, is to turn the recorder on and read the composition out loud and comment only on the "big" mistakes. This then becomes a listening exercise for the student. The grade for the composition is not given until after the student has listened to all of his teacher's comments, which seems to solve the problem of lack of attention mentioned above. Phillips feels that the most important advantage of this method of correcting themes is that it is personal. The student feels that his teacher is speaking directly to him. In short, individualized correcting. An alternative—even more personal—is to correct papers with each student.

X. Programed Instruction

108. BARRUTIA, RICHARD
     "Computerized Foreign Language Instruction," *Hisp*, 53
     (September, 1970), 361-371.

This article presents a description of a fully developed computerized
program for Spanish, first outlined by the author in 1964 [See No. 109].
This more sophisticated program incorporates an audio component in the
student terminals and eliminates the use of a typewriter terminal to
accomplish all the feedback. The basic change in the structure meant a
change in the hardware. The key problems in developing a functioning
device, however, involved the use of the computer as a language-teaching
machine rather than any impediments in overcoming technical limitations.
That is, although some CAI (Computer Assisted Instruction) concepts
concerning FL learning are in keeping with sound linguistic and
psychological theories, the programmer found that the working nature of
the machinery's component parts lessened the teaching efficiency of the
operation. In order to assure that the program determine the shape of the
device, and not vice versa, the software was emphasized as much as
possible.

The hardware consists of a "computerized" tape recorder with eight
branching tracks containing remedial work specific to the student's errors.
The response capabilities of this intrinsic device include the ability to
grade the learner's input and activate the coordinate slide, video and
responder (written) components.

Modern Spanish is the source of the language material built into the
program. Questions followed by alternative answers constitute the learning
steps. It was found that incorrect answers could be regularly predicted and
that a degree of error gravity could be assigned to each mistake (multiple
choice item). Consistent criteria were used to grade the incorrect
alternatives. When an error is made the device moves directly to the
explanation track, which tells the student where and how he was wrong.
Instructions are clear and to the point, framed in familiar Spanish.

At the end of each instructional unit the learner records his oral
production on a separate tape. This linear type programing permits a
build-up of information adequate to meet the individual needs of each
user.

Most of the beginning learning frames are audio in format, though a
good number of items are designed to teach the written skills. In these
later frames the student has more leeway and is in fact producing language
rather than selecting from among given answers. A paper puller is
coordinated with a slide which contains sample answers and the student
can compare and correct his grammar or his spelling. Dictations can also be
handled this way. The entire program uses ninety-six eight track tape reels

and 2882 slides depicting actions, places, things and some abstract concepts and diagramed grammatical explanations.

The first time the program was offered (1968) as a regular self-instructional Spanish course, four students completed it with exceptional results (as compared with those of traditionally taught students). However, nine students experienced mixed results with the second-term course. Any conclusions would be very tenuous, owing to the small learner group and the unknown and uneven amount of time devoted to the lessons. Surprisingly, students in programed instruction sections usually became quite proficient in speaking. For one reason or another, the students in the self-instructional courses were either very successful or not at all. Written and oral examinations given at the end of the third quarter confirmed the original impression that the experimental students did as well in writing and significantly better in speaking-comprehending than the non-control group.

By the second year (1969-70) the program was in operation the instrument had undergone considerable polishing. Only the winter quarter group failed to measure up to expectations. Barrutia does not try to account for this, other than to suggest the possibility that perhaps certain types of persons will not be successful at automated self-instruction.

The real promise held by this learning approach is to be found in its flexibility, emphasis on the student's role in learning, and self-pacing feature. The author recognizes that some educators will react negatively to the advances in teaching technology, but he insists that teachers cannot afford not to investigate all possibilities. One of these is programed instruction, for which he disclaims any real danger of dehumanization. And Barrutia is much more aware than most of both sides of the question, for he has had an honest go at it, as an experienced FL teacher, a competent applied linguist and a knowledgeable programmer.

109. BARRUTIA, RICHARD
      "A Suggested Automated Branch Program for Foreign Languages," *Hisp*, 47 (May, 1964), 342-350.

The thesis of this report is that, since many teachers do not even have the time nor energy to do the things that only teachers can do, a way must be found to have the machine take over the responsibility of the "habitual behavior" the student of a FL learns. Barrutia thinks that there is no need for the teacher to fear the evils of automated teaching, that "the danger of the machines does not lie in the mechanization of the teaching process but rather in the mechanization of the teacher." The machine should free the teacher by enabling him to devote more time to the individual student and to his art of combining imagination and creativity in causing learning to take place.

Barrutia correctly points out that the language laboratory is neither a labor-saving device nor a teaching machine, merely a quality-quantity device. The objectives of the branch program described here are to teach and test FL recognition and retention, with reliance on structure practice of models. Such a program can be designed to suit the individual needs of each student. It is completely automated and receives its instructions from the student's feedback.

The program is recorded on four tracks of tape; track one holds the correct answers. This track first presents a four-line dialog, which is heard in its entirety, then only the first line (with pause for repetition), followed by the English translation which is in turn immediately followed by the Spanish version. Each succeeding line is handled in the same manner and the student finally hears the whole dialog in sequence. This procedure is repeated twice. The next step, which Barrutia calls the "accumulation" process, is designed to enable the student to memorize the dialog and produce it without cues. The learner repeats line 1, then lines 1 and 2, then 1, 2 and 3, and finally the entire dialog. Like the original presentation process, this step is repeated twice.

During both procedures the student can record his responses on the second track and compare them with the model voice. And at any time the student can stop, back up, and start again. From this point on, however, the program is automatic; the machine decides when to stop, back up, and start.

The "conversation" step follows, in which the student takes one (the second) of the two roles (parts) of the dialog. He next is instructed to initiate the conversation starting with the first line, and the machine responds with the second, in other words, the one the student originally was asked to produce. Thus, he actually performs all lines of the dialog. In this "frame" format, he imitates, compares, memorizes and responds to dialog stimuli. A quiz follows this frame sequence. The test consists of a series of multiple-choice questions, each of which is followed by the correct answer after the student has given his own choice. The machine can distinguish between the least wrong (track two) and the common wrong (track three) answers and moves backward to supply explanations and illustrations, or, in the case of a very wrong answer (track four), the machine rewinds to the beginning of the frame and the student repeats the entire section. But when the student answers correctly the machine continues along track one and he will hear an immediate reinforcement question-answer after each item he tries.

Included are sketches and diagrams of the electrical and mechanical components necessary for this program.

Barrutia envisions a comprehensive program consisting of the usual audiolingual activities, integrated into different phases, the first of which had at this writing been realized to the extent of a working model. An integrated film strip, running parallel to the tape, is intended as the final step.

The author sees no reason why education, like industry, cannot make considerable use of automation. That this has not come about merits closer investigation. Barrutia's imaginative approach is exciting and suggests the possibility for successful self-pacing individualized instruction, with a minimum of supervision.

110. ESTARELLAS, JUAN
"The Self-Instructional Foreign Language Program at Florida Atlantic University," *Hisp*, 53 (September, 1970), 371-385.

Estarellas' introductory statement is not a convincing *raison d'être* for self-instructional FL courses: "A great problem in foreign language teaching today is a surplus of students and shortage of instructors." Nonetheless, there are or at least could be situations in which programed language has advantages over the more conventional alternatives. Finding no adequate program available from the current market, the author proceeded to develop his own materials.

In addition to a discussion of the need for self-instructional FL, the author includes in his article a description of the present stage of programed instruction, its theoretical background, the objectives and content of the FAU program, the materials and equipment, the teaching and testing procedures, and an evaluation of the operation.

At the time this article was written, a program had been developed for the first three Spanish language courses and had been in use for two years. The terminal behavior includes recognition and production of about one thousand words and twelve basic syntactic structures, including about twenty derived structures. (The list of grammar points Estarellas gives is more or less in accord with the contents of the average first-year text.) The materials are presented via video and audio tapes and books. No video components accompany the frames for pronunciation and writing. Considerable attention—perhaps too much—is paid to discrimination practice on phonemic-graphemic correspondence. Much of the remainder of this linear program utilizes the video tape which has a format similar to the books. An information panel presents and explains each problem. Too many of the frames appear to rely on fill-in-the-blank responses, though pattern transformations, for example, are also used. Students might have difficulty following the strategy of the frames, as some appear to admit several possible answers. In the most advanced and complex learning situations the student has a conversation with the TV or audio tape. Questions are based on picture stories and answers are provided. Techniques other than the ones already mentioned include multiple choice, questions on readings, dialogs in which the student takes a role, and dictation.

Students who enroll for these self-instructional courses attend orientation sessions. This is essential and is the opportunity for whoever manages the program to get the participants started on the right track, for all experience with this kind of learning set-up indicates the need for careful and continued guidance.

The examinations, which can be taken at any time, are used to check the student's progress and his final level of achievement. Only grades of *A* or *B* are considered passing. The exams are graded by computer.

The 500 students who have used this program at FAU earned 70 percent *A*'s, 20 percent *B*'s and 10 percent Incompletes. Reaction of the students as expressed on questionnaires has been generally favorable. In particular they like the responsibility and the self-pacing this learning opportunity provides. Student motivation was found to be the only serious problem.

111. TURNER, RONALD C.
    "CARLOS: Computer-Assisted Instruction in Spanish," *Hisp*, 53 (May, 1970), 249-252.

CARLOS (Computer-Assisted Review Lessons on Syntax) had its origin not in pedagogical theory but in the practical homework needs of Spanish 2 students at Dartmouth College. Turner did the bulk of the programing for the time-sharing computer as well as instruct the class that made use of it.

During one term students performed some 250 lessons of written homework on the computer. The format of the operation is quite simple. After the student identifies himself in type, he requests a lesson, which he goes through up to the point he chooses (and after home study). The user can have his work graded at any time and can use the teletyped results for further review.

The programed exercises were adapted from the Castellano and Brown *A New Shorter Spanish Review Grammar* (Scribner), and each lesson contains page references to the original. When the student does not give a correct answer, or has a false start, CARLOS is able to give specific advice. After the second chapter the instructions are entirely in Spanish. The format of each lesson allows for two possible correct answers, two anticipated errors, and for the really lost student, a general comment on the problem at hand.

An attempt was made to evaluate CARLOS, using both the SAT Verbal Aptitude scores and those for the CEEB Spanish Reading Examination. Students who used the computer missed 36 percent fewer points on a special section of a final examination than did a group of non-participants who studied the same grammar but in other ways. Furthermore, the CARLOS group came out significantly better on the CEEB scores. Unexpectedly, they averaged 25 points lower on the SAT verbal score than the non-experimental students. The limited scope of the experiment and the teacher/student variables preclude any firm empirical claims.

An attitude survey revealed that generally positive responses were given by the learners who completed the course with the aid of CARLOS. All in all, the system was judged flexible, practical, economical and successful. The complete report of the project is on file with the Educational Resources Information Center and available through its ERIC Document Reproduction Service.

XI. Testing

112. ANDRADE, MANUEL, JOHN L. HAYMAN, JR.,
     and JAMES T. JOHNSON, JR.
     "Measurement of Listening Comprehension in Elementary-School
     Spanish Instruction," *ESJ*, 64 (October, 1963), 84-93.

Describes listening comprehension tests developed for the Denver-
Stanford Project, a FLES program begun in 1960 and supported in part by
the U.S. Office of Education under Title VII of the NDEA. The challenge
for the test makers was to produce reliable instruments to evaluate the
achievement of 6,000 pupils who were studying beginning FL.

Instruction in Spanish began in the fifth grade and was entirely
audiolingual. Though English was used on occasion, translation and formal
grammar (including word list study) was shunned. Since no written
materials were used, devising valid tests for these students posed real
problems. Nonetheless, it was decided that 1) The tests should correspond
closely to the content and format of the material taught; 2) Only Spanish
would be used; 3) No reading or writing of Spanish would be required;
4) All test items should be in a Spanish language context (i.e., no
vocabulary, etc., out of context); and 5) The test items should
discriminate.

To assure uniformity the tests were administered via television.
Controlled vocabulary and grammar as functional usage were emphasized.
Especially stressed were concordance and verb forms; syntax was not. The
first-semester midterm exam consisted of 50 items chosen from an original
153 which had been pretested with 200 pupils. A mean of 70 percent
correct answers and a standard deviation of 5 were sought. Eight types of
items were used, including single-picture (with multiple oral stimuli),
multiple-picture, and correct/incorrect alternative types for article
agreement, logical rejoinder statements, identification, adjective agreement, word order, and verb forms. For these last types the students
answered *sí* or *no*, or circled answer 1 or 2. Though the test results were
generally satisfactory, the team of test writers improved the validity for a
first-semester and a second-semester final. The average biserial correlation
coefficients for the picture items and that of the non-picture ones for each
of these finals were, respectively, .570/.471 and .570/.295. Correct
answers averaged the desired 70 percent. Since the picture test items
provided substantially higher discrimination, especially for the second-
semester exam, they alone were used thereafter in the Denver-Stanford
Project.

Although the teachers responsible for the tests described in this report
established what appear to be acceptable criteria for constructing these
tests, no indication is given as to teacher reaction. But since course content
(including, presumably, the teaching method) was carefully considered and

the pretesting allowed improved reliability, the individual results should have corroborated whatever expectations the participating teachers held.

113. HOGE, HENRY W.
"Testing in the Language Laboratory: A Laboratory Experiment in Spanish Pronunciation," *Lang*, 42 (March, 1959), 147-152.

Reports the results of a language lab experiment at Indiana University. Hoge first points out the advantages in using the lab for testing. Uniformity of test conditions can be assured, an unfamiliar voice can serve as item stimulus for all students in multi-section courses, and students can adjust what they hear for volume and clarity. The use of headsets removes most of the disturbance common to the classroom situation. On the other hand, scores will likely be lower on tests administered in the lab because the student cannot rely on facial expression, including lip movement and gestures of the test giver.

In this experiment the author wanted to measure the correlation between the student's ability to pronounce Spanish and his mastery of oral comprehension. The participating students attended a half-hour lab session each week during their first-semester Spanish course (1957-58). Scores were obtained for achievement on dictation and comprehension exercises, which more or less repeated class content. Not surprisingly, the results were disappointing, and a special 12-day review course on pronunciation was created. Attendance at the 31 half-hour periods was voluntary. Supposedly the students did not know their performances were in fact part of test exercises.

Shortly before and after the special review course was offered, a departmental aural comprehension quiz and a dictation test were given to all elementary students. Thirty-eight completed the entire laboratory course, with test information for 33 of these. When compared with those students who did not volunteer for the experiment, a decided improvement is noted for those who did. This difference can. only be accounted for in terms of the additional practice. We are assured that the volunteer group as a whole did not include better or more ambitious students.

Hoge describes the kind of dictation format used and shows how the test data can be analyzed (as given in his tabulation charts).

He suggests that the student who "acquires a reasonable accurate mental sound-picture of Spanish words" will comprehend better than his classmate who does not. And there are other implications, equally questionable. Nonetheless, the data produced by this laboratory test tend to support the theory that (early) practice given to pronunciation will increase the student's ability to understand the spoken language.

114. HOLTON, JAMES S.
"The Proficiency Ladder," *Hisp*, 46 (December, 1963), 781-785.

Reactions prompted by the author's observation of participants in NDEA Language Institutes. He found that these teachers were not deriving optimum benefit from their laboratory experience in becoming more proficient in the language because needed individual work was not possible. All participants were made to perform all drills, etc., regardless of the deficiencies of each. In fact, individual diagnosis and prescription for remedial work were usually lacking.

Holton thinks that the lab could have provided an excellent opportunity for each learner to progress at his own pace, after careful diagnosis of the weak areas. In this paper the author describes a technique he successfully used at the Spanish Institute at Fresno State College, summer, 1962.

Holton calls his approach the "Proficiency Ladder." The rationale behind it is that armed with a means of evaluating his own proficiency, ways to increase it, and a goal to aim at, the student can operate on his own with a minimum of outside direction and a maximum of efficiency.

The Proficiency Ladder is made up of a series of grammatical areas (twenty-seven in all, beginning with present tense verbs and ending with variation drills for complex adjective agreement), for each of which there is an oral lab test and a series of appropriate drills. The "goal to shoot at" is provided by posting these test results and encouraging all the participants to pass the tests before their institute experience comes to an end. The author noticed increased interest and a healthy rivalry.

He recognizes that his grammatical ladder, based on *Modern Spanish* (first edition), is incomplete and could stand some adjustments. The sample pattern drills from a part of the test are typical in quality of those for which Holton has become deservedly well-known. Characteristically they embody simple, clear instructions, the right kinds of stimuli (minimal, when possible), and productive structures. Listed are factors a writer of oral tests should bear in mind if he is to arrive at workable procedures for the different kinds of formats.

The author points out that while the testee should be given sufficient information for his answer, care must be taken so that the answer not be telegraphed. He also prefers that translations be avoided, though he admits that it is not always easy to write good items in the target language for certain points of grammar, especially where binary contrasts exist.

The tests are to be evaluated solely on the basis of the particular element tested in each item. Suggestions are given for simplifying the scoring procedure.

Obviously, the tests described in this presentation could be used in the usual high school or college programs. Their particular advantage over other test types is their value in pinpointing individual problem areas.

115. WILKINS, GEORGE W., JR. and E. LEE HOFFMAN
      "The Use of Cognates in Testing Pronunciation," *LL*, 14:1-2 (1964), 39-43.

Looking at cognates as problems of pronunciation rather than problems of vocabulary, the authors have endeavored to test for correlations between student level and ability to cope with the phonetics of cognate words. Whether or not one accepts their statement that "the applied linguist recognizes cognates as trouble spots, and takes pains to avoid their introduction before a reasonably good foundation in pronunciation and writing can be attained...," it is to be anticipated that the general degree of phonologic proficiency should concord with the student's oral control of cognates.

One assumption underlying this test is that the learner will especially have trouble with cognates presented out of context. And the use of a simple list of carefully selected words solves the usual problem of eliciting uniform responses from a group of testees.

Data were collected for this experimental test from second semester sections of elementary and intermediate Spanish at Tulane University. In order to assure spontaneous production, the particular sounds to be checked were concealed. Only one sound for each word was considered. The student read each word from the list and then imitated a native speaker's version. Results of these tests, showing ranges of differences among the various course levels, are given in graphical representations. This kind of test was found to be a reliable index of the different achievement levels among the various groups. The authors also report in progress a near-spontaneous production test with cognates.

116. WOODFORD, PROTASE E.
      "Testing Procedures," in *A Handbook for Teachers of Spanish and Portuguese*, edited by Donald D. Walsh. Lexington, Mass.: D. C. Heath and Co., 1969, 89-107.

Most of the familiar test formats are presented in this article:

1) Classroom tests. The purposes to be served by class quizzes include (a) the teacher's awareness of the student's progress, (b) exposure of weaknesses, (c) motivation, (d) test fright reduction, and (e) objective evidence for grading. Tests should be introduced no later than the first week of instruction. The idea here is that it doesn't matter what is evaluated, students will study for tests and this justifies them. Both oral and written formats are possible, and the language lab can be used.

2) Listening tests. The two major types of listening items are those with both stimulus and answer choices spoken and those with only stimulus spoken, the answer choices being printed or depicted visually. Woodford puts forth some of the necessary criteria for make-up and procedure. He insists that the emphasis must be on hearing, not reading—all the answer alternatives should be readily understood. "Picture" questions are suggested, but the author does not explore many of the possibilities. He also fails to recognize any oral stimulus other than the question and identification of elements from read statements.

3) Reading tests. For these both stimulus and response choices are printed. Their structure can parallel those of the comprehension tests. Unlike the listening test, which usually involves only recognition, a writing test can evaluate production.

4) Reading comprehension tests. The trick here is to avoid a repetition of similar or the same wording in the question as that found in the reading passage. Familiar material should be avoided.

5) Speaking tests. The student may be asked to produce a spoken response to either a visual or an auditory stimulus. Unless the teacher insists on a "full sentence" answer (Should he?), the pupil's response cannot be delimited and there is a real problem of objectifying evaluations of the answers. Woodford wonders if it might not be best to first determine the desired response and work back to the stimulus that will elicit it. Scoring criteria are discussed. The author advocates using visuals for this quiz type. Ordinary drills can also test speaking ability, as can the dialog framework (which actually tests comprehension, too).

6) Writing tests. This can be anything from a one-word fill-in to an involved essay. Writing can be defined in several ways, but one thing which it is not is merely copying a dialog from memory. This only tests recall and spelling.

The author also discusses test construction, standardized tests and advanced placement tests. His suggestions are for the most part quite practical. He lists information sources as well as specific available commercial tests.

This article is fine as far as it goes, but much more can be said on the subject. For example, can and should testing be also teaching? How can the teacher know he is evaluating objectively? When the testee is given choice answers, how should the wrong ones be incorrect? Should teachers do more teaching and less quizzing? Can or need the skills be separated in tests?

XII. Miscellaneous

117. BULL, WILLIAM E.
   "Spanish Word Counts: Theory and Practice," *MLJ*, 34 (January, 1950), 18-26.

This paper proposes to study the validity of frequency word counts and their consequences for the learner of a FL. Making his own count and comparing the results with those of several widely-known lists (notably, Milton A. Buchanan's *A Graded Spanish Word Book*, 1927, and Hayward Keniston's *A Standard List of Spanish Words and Idioms*, 1941), Bull found the results to be inconsistent, that the data were not repeated in either of three tabulations. In fact, Keniston's "rare" and "common" adjectives showed up in this later count with about the same relative frequency, in a wide variety of contemporary Spanish sources. One word count, therefore, will not predict the results of another, regardless of how large the sampling, because too many of the words appear in only half or less of the literary or oral samples. Furthermore, a shift in subject matter is likely to make rare words common and common words rare.

The author feels that high frequency and range have very little meaning for the student until the words assume a given spacing (i.e., a word's probable number of occurrences per lesson). Bull's calculations show that a college student of Spanish could acquire a reading knowledge of the language without ever encountering a majority of the common words, not to mention all their meanings.

The author's concern is that the learner's real problem is the words he does *not* know, which point is overlooked in word-count philosophy. The cold fact is that the student who knows all the words on Keniston's list knows only 50 percent of the vocabulary he must learn to read with ease, an average of only 13.9 words per page. Bull can find no way to increase the probability that a frequency curve will reliably represent the source from which the words are taken. The average textbook all but guarantees the appearance of the commonest words, which the student over-learns. But he receives the least help when he needs it most, when he meets the less frequent words, which are inevitably under-taught.

The author's conclusion is that the word-count system assures that the student will be carefully taught the easy words, but is left to learn the rest, the most difficult ones, on his own. Frequency counts should be used to isolate the very rare words (not to be taught), the very common ones (to be under-taught), and those lexical items which fall in-between, which can be spaced throughout the first year of language study. This strategy makes a lot of sense.

118. GREEN, JERALD R.
     A Gesture Inventory for the Teaching of Spanish. Philadelphia: The Center for Curriculum Development, Inc., 1968. xiii + 114 pp.

A systematically organized and well documented list of gestures used by Spanish speakers in Spain and Spanish America. Each of the gestures is abundantly illustrated and accurately interpreted. Sources for the inventory include native speakers and contemporary fiction.

Especially noteworthy in this collection is the author's success in classifying his material. Green has done an admirable job of solving the problem of classification and the excellent index will serve the user as he works his way through some two hundred gestures.

Chapter I is introductory; Chapter II presents the nature and limitations of kinesic research; Chapter III is a survey of gesture research; Chapter IV studies the kinesics of a foreign culture; Chapter V presents the gestures of the modern Spanish culture; and Chapter VI discusses the role of gestures in the teaching of Spanish. Sample dialogs are given to exemplify usage of some of the gestures. A selected bibliography completes the study.

Though not all gestures are described, most of the familiar and useful ones are and teachers of Spanish and individuals in other disciplines will find this attractively illustrated and carefully documented volume a welcome addendum to the field.

119. KNOWLTON, JOHN F.
     "The Untranslatable: Translation as a Critical Tool," *Hisp*, 50 (March, 1967), 125-128.

Although Knowlton brings to light no general or basic truths about the nature of translation not already known to serious practitioners of the art, he provides the FL teacher with some useful pointers or cautions well worth knowing.

To exemplify some bad or at least inadequate translations, the author quotes from sample English versions of Bécquer, the *Vida del buscón, Don Quijote,* and the poetry of García Lorca and Antonio Machado. These are shown as typical imperfect translations, whose kind or degree of deviation from the original ranges from elements of factual content to subtle "flavor." In the case of prose, the author finds the faulty translation often without the same "rhythmic movement" of the Spanish selection, and the poetry, changed because of a combination of linguistic factors involving word order, word length, stress, and the like.

For those prose passages to which a specific kind of flow of speech is essential in maintaining the stylistic essence, translation can at times distort the original because of the "natural inadequacy" of English (meaning its different rhythmic patterns). Idiomatic expressions, word play, and phraseology are familiar stubborn obstacles for the translator.

When word order and poetic imagery are sacrificed in order to retain the rhythm, an examination of the original can often reveal to the student the particular genius of the translated lines.

In this short but incisive look at translation, the author has ably demonstrated the usefulness of a linguistic approach to the basic problems. His suggestions regarding different kinds of problems for untranslatable prose and poetry are valid and argue for more serious studies applying linguistics to a deeper understanding of precisely what is involved.

.

Appendix

I. BIBLIOGRAPHIES

Alden, Douglas W. *Materials List for Use by Teachers of Modern Foreign Languages.* New York: Modern Language Association, 1959.

Bibliographies of Books in Foreign Languages. Vol. 2 (Spanish), Grade 1 through junior college. Dade County (Florida) Foreign Language Bibliographic Committee, 1964.

Birkmaier, Emma M. and Dale L. Lange. *A Selective Bibliography on the Teaching of Foreign Languages, 1920-1966.* New York: MLA Materials Center, 1968.

Brady, Agnes Marie. "Materials for Teaching Spanish in Elementary and Junior High Schools" (rev.), *Hispania*, 45 (September, 1962), 511-536.

Coleman, Algernon. *An Analytical Bibliography of Modern Language Teaching*, Vol. 3, 1937-1942. New York: King's Crown Press, 1949.

de la Portilla, Marta and Thomas Colchie. *Textbooks in Spanish and Portuguese: A Descriptive Bibliography.* New York: MLA/ERIC, 1972.

Dingwall, William Orr. *Transformational Generative Grammar: A Bibliography.* Washington, D.C.: Center for Applied Linguistics, 1965.

Eaton, Esther M., Mary E. Hayes and Helen L. O'Leary. *Source Materials for Secondary School Teachers of Foreign Languages.* Washington, D.C.: U.S. Department of Health, Education and Welfare, 1966.

Ferguson, Charles A. and William A. Stewart, eds. *Linguistic Reading Lists for Teachers of Modern Languages: French, German, Italian, Russian, Spanish.* Washington, D.C.: Center for Applied Linguistics, 1963.

Gage, William W. *Contrastive Studies in Linguistics: A Bibliographical Checklist.* Washington, D.C.: Center for Applied Linguistics, 1965.

García Blanco, M. and Antonio Tovar. "Bibliografía de estudios lingüísticos publicados en España (1939-1946)," *Cultura Neolatina* (Rome), 6 (1946), 231-254.

Gonsalves, Julia, *et al. Bibliography of Spanish Materials for Children: Kindergarten through Grade Six.* Sacramento: California State Department of Education, 1971.

Hall, Pauline Cook. *A Bibliography of Spanish Linguistics: Articles in Serial Publications. Language* Supplement No. 54. Baltimore: Waverly Press, October-December, 1956.

Hammer, John H., in consultation with Frank A. Rice. *A Bibliography of Contrastive Linguistics.* Washington, D.C.: Center for Applied Linguistics, 1965.

Johnston, Marjorie C. and Ilo Remer. *References on Foreign Languages in the Elementary School.* Washington, D.C.: U.S. Department of Health, Education and Welfare, 1957.

Keesee, Elizabeth. *References on Foreign Languages in the Elementary School.* Washington, D.C.: U.S. Department of Health, Education and Welfare, 1963.

Mildenberger, Andrea S., et al. *ERIC Documents on the Teaching of Foreign Languages: Lists 1-4.* New York: MLA/ERIC, 1971.

Miller, Minnie M. *Bibliography of Material for Use in Spanish Classes* (rev. ed.). Emporia: Kansas State Teachers College, 1965.

Nichols, Madaline W. *A Bibliographical Guide to Materials on American Spanish.* Cambridge, Mass.: Harvard University Press, 1941.

Nostrand, Howard Lee, et al. *Research on Language Teaching: An Annotated International Bibliography, 1945-1964* (2nd ed., rev.). Seattle and London: University of Washington Press, 1965.

Ollmann, Mary J., ed. *MLA Selective List of Materials for Use by Teachers of Modern Foreign Languages in Elementary and Secondary Schools.* New York: Modern Language Association, 1962. [A 1964 Supplement for Spanish and Portuguese is available from the MLA Materials Center.]

Rice, Frank and Allene Guss. *Information Sources in Linguistics: A Bibliographical Handbook.* Washington, D.C.: Center for Applied Linguistics, 1965.

Rice, Winthrop H. "An Annotated Bibliography of Modern Language Methodology," *The Modern Language Journal*, 30 (May, 1964), 290-308.

Robinson, Janet O. *An Annotated Bibliography of Modern Language Teaching: Books and Articles, 1946-1967.* London: Oxford University Press, 1969.

Rutherford, Phillip R. *A Bibliography of American Doctoral Dissertations in Linguistics, 1900-1964.* Washington, D.C.: Center for Applied Linguistics, 1968.

Solé, Carlos A. *Bibliografía sobre el español en América (1920-1967).* Washington, D.C.: Georgetown University Press, 1970.

UNESCO. *A Bibliography on the Teaching of Modern Languages.* Paris: UNESCO, 1955.

Van Eenenaam, Evelyn. "Annotated Bibliography of Modern Language Methodology for 1950," *The Modern Language Journal*, 36 (January), 39-56. [Also, by same author annually in *MLJ*, 1953-1961.]

Wible, Gerald L. *Source Guide to 5000 Aids for Teaching Spanish.* Allentown, Pa.: Wible Language Institute, 1962.

Zamora Vicente, A. "Bibliografía lingüística española (1939-1947)," *Revista portuguêsa de filologia.* Suplemento bibliográfico (Coimbra), 1 (1951), 226-247.

II. SPANISH PHONOLOGY

Alarcos Llorach, Emilio. *Fonología española.* Madrid: Editorial Gredos, 1965.

———. "El sistema fonológico español," *Revista de filología española,* 33 (July-December, 1948), 265-296.

Alonso, Amado. "La *ll* y sus alteraciones en España y América," *Estudios dedicados a Menéndez Pidal,* II. Madrid: CSIC, 1951, 41-89.

——. "Una ley fonológica del español," *Hispanic Review,* 13 (April, 1945), 91-101.

Anthony, Ann. "A Structural Approach to the Analysis of Spanish Intonation," *Language Learning,* 1 (July, 1948), 24-31.

Bolinger, Dwight L., "English Prosodic Stress and Spanish Sentence Order," *Hispania,* 37 (May, 1954), 152-156.

Bowen, J. Donald. "A Comparison of the Intonation Patterns of English and Spanish," *Hispania,* 39 (March, 1956), 30-35.

———, and Robert P. Stockwell. "The Phonemic Interpretation of Semivowels in Spanish," *Language,* 31 (1955), 236-240.

———. "A Further Note on Spanish Semivowels," *Language,* 32 (1956), 290-292.

Campbell, Richard J. *Phonological Analyses of Spanish.* Unpublished Dissertation (Illinois, 1967).

Canfield, D. Lincoln. "Trends in American Castilian," *Hispania,* 50 (December, 1967), 912-918.

Fitzgibbon, J. P. and J. Merino. *Spanish Pronunciation Illustrated.* New York: Cambridge University Press, 1963.

Foster, David W. "A Contrastive Note on Stress in English and Equivalent Stresses in Spanish," *International Review of Applied Linguistics,* 6 (August, 1968), 257-266.

García, Ernest F. *Interference by Textual Stimuli on Selected Elements of Spanish Pronunciation.* Unpublished Dissertation (California, Los Angeles, 1966).

Gili Gaya, Samuel. *Elementos de fonética general* (4th ed.). Madrid: Editorial Gredos, 1961.

Harris, James W. *Spanish Phonology.* Cambridge, Mass.: M.I.T. Press, 1969.

Lado, Robert. "A Comparison of the Sound Systems of English and Spanish," *Hispania*, 39 (March, 1956), 26-29.

Navarro Tomás, Tomás. *Estudios de fonología española.* Syracuse, New York: Syracuse University Press, 1946.

———. *Manual de entonación española* (2nd ed.). New York: Hispanic Institute in the United States, 1948.

———. "Palabras sin acento," *Revista de filología española*, 12 (1925), 335-375.

———. "La pronunciación en el *ALPI*," *Hispania*, 47 (December, 1964), 716-721.

———. *Studies in Spanish Phonology* (translated by R. D. Abraham). Coral Gables: University of Miami Press, 1968.

———, and Aurelio M. Espinosa. *A Primer of Spanish Pronunciation.* Boston: Sanborn and Co., 1926.

Predmore, Richard L. "Notes on Spanish Consonant Phonemes," *Hispanic Review*, 14 (April, 1946), 169-172.

Quilis, Antonio and Joseph A. Fernández. *Curso de fonética y fonología españolas para estudiantes angloamericanos* (2nd ed.). Madrid: CSIC, 1966.

Resnick, Melvyn C. "Dialect Zones and Automatic Dialect Identification in Latin American Spanish," *Hispania*, 52 (October, 1969), 553-568.

Saporta, Sol. "A Note on Spanish Semivowels," *Language*, 32 (1956), 287-290.

———, and Rita Cohen. "The Distribution and Relative Frequency of Spanish Diphthongs," *Romance Philology*, 11 (May, 1958), 371-377.

———, and Heles Contreras. *A Phonological Grammar of Spanish.* Seattle: University of Washington Press, 1962.

———, and Donald Olson. "Classification of Intervocalic Clusters," *Language*, 34 (1958), 261-266.

Skelton, Robert B. "The Pattern of Spanish Vowel Sounds," *International Journal of Applied Linguistics*, 7 (August, 1969), 231-237.

Stockwell, Robert P., J. Donald Bowen and I. Silva-Fuenzalida. "Spanish Juncture and Intonation," *Language*, 32 (1956), 641-665.

Trager, George L. "The Phonemes of Castilian Spanish," *Travaux du Cercle linguistique de Prague*, 8 (1939), 217-222.

III. SPANISH GRAMMAR

Alarcos Llorach, Emilio. *Estudios de gramática funcional del español.* Madrid: Gredos, 1970.

———. *Gramática estructural.* Madrid: Editorial Gredos, 1951.

———. "Sobre la estructura del verbo español," *Boletín de la Biblioteca de Menéndez Pelayo* (Santander), 25 (1949), 50-83.

Alonso, Amado. *Estudios lingüísticos: temas hispano-americanos.* Madrid: Editorial Gredos, 1961.

———. *Gramática castellana* (8th ed.). Buenos Aires: Editorial Losada, 1947.

Alonso, Martín. *Gramática del español contemporáneo.* Madrid: Ediciones Guadarrama, 1968.

Anderson, James M. "The Morphophonemics of Gender in Spanish Nouns," *Lingua*, 10 (1961), 285-296.

Babcock, Sandra S. *The Syntax of Spanish Reflexive Verbs.* The Hague: Mouton, 1970.

Beinhauer, Werner. *El español coloquial.* Madrid: Editorial Gredos, 1963.

Bello, Andrés and Rufino José Cuervo. *Gramática de la lengua castellana* (new ed.). Buenos Aires: Ediciones Anaconda, 1945.

Bente, Thomas O. "Observations on *igual* and the *igual que, igual a* Construction," *Hispania*, 52 (March, 1969), 77-79.

Bolinger, Dwight L. "The Comparison of Inequality in Spanish," *Language*, 26 (1950), 28-62.

———. "Addenda to the Comparison of Inequality in Spanish," *Language*, 29 (1953), 62-66.

———. "Adjective Position Again," *Hispania*, 55 (March, 1972), 91-94.

———. "Discontinuity of the Spanish Conjunctive Pronoun," *Language*, 25 (1949), 253-260.

———. "Linear Modification in Spanish," *Publications of the Modern Language Association of America*, 67 (December, 1952), 1117-1144.

———. "Meaningful Word Order in Spanish," *Boletín de Filología* (Universidad de Chile), 8 (1954-1955), 45-46.

———. "More on *ser* and *estar*," *The Modern Language Journal*, 28 (March, 1944), 233-238.

———. "The Relative Importance of Grammatical Items," *Hispania*, 38 (September, 1955), 261-264.

———. "Retained Objects in Spanish," *Hispania*, 33 (August, 1950), 237-239.

Buchanan, Milton A. *A Spanish Word List.* Toronto: University of Toronto Press, 1941.

Bull, William E. "New Principles for Some Spanish Equivalents of *to be*," *Hispania*, 25 (May, 1942), 433-443.

———. "Related Functions of *haber* and *estar*," *The Modern Language Journal*, 27 (February, 1943), 119-123.

———. "Spanish Adjective Position: The Theory of Valence Classes," *Hispania*, 37 (March, 1954), 32-38.

———. *Time, Tense and the Verb*. Berkeley and Los Angeles: University of California Press, 1960.

———. *A Visual Grammar of Spanish: Manual of Instructions.* Los Angeles: U.C.L.A. Extension, 1966.

———, Allison Gronberg and James Abbott. "Subject Position in Contemporary Spanish," *Hispania*, 35 (May, 1952), 185-188.

———, *et al.* "Modern Spanish Verb-form Frequencies," *Hispania*, 30 (November, 1947), 451-466.

Cárdenas, Daniel N. "The Application of Linguistics to the Teaching of Spanish," *Hispania*, 40 (December, 1957), 455-460.

Cressey, William W. "Relative Adverbs in Spanish: A Transformational Analysis," *Language*, 44 (1968), 487-500.

———. *A Transformational Analysis of the Relative Clause in Urban Mexican Spanish.* Unpublished Dissertation (Illinois, 1966).

Criado de Val, Manuel. *Fisonomía del idioma español.* Madrid: Aguilar, 1957.

———. *Gramática española.* Madrid: Sociedad Anónima Española de Traductores y Autores, 1958.

———. *Sintaxis del verbo español moderno, Revista de filología española,* Añejo 41, 1948.

———. *Síntesis de morfología española.* Madrid: CSIC, 1952.

———. *El verbo español.* Madrid: Sociedad Anónima Española de Traductores y Autores, 1969.

Cuervo, Rufino José. *Diccionario de construcción y régimen de la lengua castellana.* Bogotá: Instituto Caro y Cuervo, 1962.

deGorog, Ralph. "Trends in Spanish Vocabulary (1913-1963)," *Hispania*, 48 (October, 1965), 645-667.

Dowdle, Harold L. "Observations on the Uses of *a* and *de* in Spanish," *Hispania*, 50 (May, 1967), 329-334.

Falk, Julia S. *Nominalizations in Spanish.* (Studies in Linguistics and Language Learning, 5.) Seattle: University of Washington, 1968.

Fish, Gordon T. "*A* with Spanish Direct Object," *Hispania*, 50 (March, 1967), 80-85.

———. "The Indirect Object and the Redundant Construction," *Hispania*, 51 (December, 1968), 862-866.

———. "The Neglected Tenses: *Hube hecho*, Indicative *-ra, -re*," *Hispania*, 46 (March, 1963), 138-142.

————. "The Redundant Construction in Standard Spanish," *Hispania*, 41 (September, 1958), 324-331.

————. "Subjunctive of Fact," *Hispania*, 46 (May, 1963), 375-381.

Foley, James A. *Spanish Morphology*. Unpublished Dissertation (M.I.T., 1965).

Foster, David W. *"Sintáctica esiva del inglés y español,"* *Hispania*, 52 (September, 1969), 419-426.

————. "Spanish So-called Impersonal Sentences," *Anthropological Linguistics*, 12 (January, 1970), 1-9.

García de Diego, Vincente. *Manual de dialectología española* (2nd ed.). Madrid: Ediciones Cultura Hispánica, 1959.

Gerrard, A. Bryson and José de Heras Heras. *Beyond the Dictionary in Spanish: A Handbook of Colloquial Usage*. New York: Funk and Wagnalls, 1964.

Gili y Gaya, Samuel. *Curso superior de sintaxis española* (8th ed.). Barcelona: Publicaciones y Ediciones Spes, 1961.

————. *Diccionario de sinónimos* (2nd ed.). Barcelona: Publicaciones y Ediciones Spes, 1961.

Goldin, Mark G. *Spanish Case and Function*. Washington, D.C.: Georgetown University Press, 1968.

Gooch, Anthony. *Diminutive, Augmentative, and Pejorative Suffixes in Modern Spanish*. Oxford, New York: Pergamon Press, 1967.

Hadlich, Roger L. *A Transformational Grammar of Spanish*. Englewood Cliffs, New Jersey: Prentice-Hall, Inc., 1971.

Hernández de Mendoza, Cecilia. *Introducción a la estilística*. Bogotá: Instituto Caro y Cuervo, 1962.

Iannucci, James E. *Lexical Number in Spanish Nouns with Reference to Their English Equivalents*. Philadelphia: University of Pennsylvania Press, 1952.

Irving, T. B. "The Spanish Reflexive and the Verbal Sentence," *Hispania*, 35 (August, 1952), 305-309.

Jensen, John B. "The Feature [± Human] as a Constraint on the Occurrence of Third-Person Subject Pronouns in Spanish," *Hispania*, 56 (March, 1973), 116-122.

Kahane, Henry R. and Angelina Pietrangeli, eds. *Descriptive Studies in Spanish Grammar*. Urbana: University of Illinois Press, 1954.

————. *Structural Studies on Spanish Themes*. Urbana: University of Illinois Press, 1959.

Kany, Charles E. *American-Spanish Euphemisms*. Berkeley: University of California Press, 1960.

————. *American-Spanish Semantics*. Berkeley: University of California Press, 1960.

                             Critical Bibliography

––––. *American-Spanish Syntax* (2nd ed.). Chicago: University of Chicago Press, 1951.

Kendrich, Edith Johnston. *A Semantic Study of Cognates in Spanish and English.* Urbana: University of Illinois Press, 1943.

Keniston, Hayward. *A Spanish Idiom List.* New York: Macmillan, 1929.

––––. *Spanish Syntax List.* New York: Henry Holt, 1937.

––––. *A Standard List of Spanish Words and Idioms.* Boston: D. C. Heath and Co., 1941.

Klein, Philip W. *Modal Auxiliaries in Spanish.* (Studies in Linguistics and Language Learning, 4.) Seattle: University of Washington, 1968.

Lackstrom, John E. *Pro-forms in the Spanish Noun Phrase.* (Studies in Linguistics and Language Learning, 3.) Seattle: University of Washington, 1967.

Leuschel, Donald A. *Spanish Verb Morphology.* Unpublished Dissertation (Indiana, 1960).

López, María Luisa. *Problemas y métodos en el análisis de preposiciones.* Madrid: Editorial Gredos, 1970.

Lorenzo y Criado, Emilio. *El español de hoy.* Madrid: Editorial Gredos, 1966.

Lozano, Anthony G. "Subjunctives, Transformations and Features in Spanish," *Hispania*, 55 (March, 1972), 76-90.

Malaret, Augusto. *Diccionario de americanismos* (3rd ed.). Buenos Aires: Emecé Editores, 1946.

Marín, Diego. "El uso de *tú* y *usted* en el español actual," *Hispania*, 55 (December, 1972), 904-908.

McWilliams, Ralph Dale. "The Adverb in Colloquial Spanish," in Kahane, Henry R. and Angelina Pietrangeli, eds., *Descriptive Studies in Spanish Grammar.* Urbana: University of Illinois Press, 1954, 73-137.

Miller, J. Dale. *1,000 Spanish Idioms.* Provo, Utah: Brigham Young University Press, 1970.

Murphy, Spencer L., Jr. "A Description of Noun Suffixes in Colloquial Spanish," in Kahane, Henry R. and Angelina Pietrangeli, eds., *Descriptive Studies in Spanish Grammar.* Urbana: University of Illinois Press, 1954, 1-48.

Nunn, Marshall E. and Herbert A. Van Scoy. *Glossary of Related Spanish-English Words.* Tuscaloosa: University of Alabama Press, 1949.

Pottier, Bernard. *Gramática del español.* Versión española de Antonio Quilis. Madrid: Ediciones Alcalá, 1970.

Rallides, Charles. "The Temporal Element of the Non-Finite Verb Forms in Spanish," *Hispania*, 51 (March, 1968), 132-136.

Ramsey, Marathon M. *A Textbook of Modern Spanish*, revised by Robert K. Spaulding. New York: Henry Holt, 1956.

Real Academia Española. *Gramática de la lengua española* (rev. of 1931 ed.). Madrid: Espasa-Calpe, 1959.

Ringo, Elbert Winfred. "The Position of the Noun Modifier in Colloquial Spanish," in Kahane, Henry R. and Angelina Pietrangeli, eds., *Descriptive Studies in Spanish Grammar*. Urbana: University of Illinois Press, 1954, 49-72.

Rodríguez Herrera, Esteban. *Observaciones acerca del género de los nombres*. 2 vols. Havana: Editorial Lex, 1947.

Saporta, Sol. "Morpheme Alternants in Spanish," in Kahane, Henry R. and Angelina Pietrangeli, eds., *Structural Studies on Spanish Themes*. Urbana: University of Illinois Press, 1959, 19-162.

———. "On the Expression of Gender in Spanish," *Romance Philology*, 15 (February, 1962), 279-284.

———. "Spanish Person Markers," *Language*, 35 (1959), 612-615.

Schevill, Isabel Magaña. *Manual of Basic Spanish Constructions*. Palo Alto: Stanford University Press, 1970.

Seco, Manuel. *Diccionario de dudas y dificultades de la lengua española*. Madrid: Aguilar, 1964.

Seco Sánchez, Rafael. *Manual de gramática española* (7th ed.). Madrid: Aguilar, 1965.

Spaulding, Robert K. *Syntax of the Spanish Verb*. New York: Henry Holt, 1931.

Staubach, Charles N. "Current Variations in the Past Indicative Uses of the *-ra* Form," *Hispania*, 29 (1946), 355-362.

Stevens, Claire. *A Characterization of Spanish Nouns and Adjectives*. (Studies in Linguistics and Language Learning, 2.) Seattle: University of Washington, 1966.

Stevenson, C. H. *The Spanish Language Today*. New York: Hillary House, 1971.

Thomsen, Eugene V. *The Generation and Surface Ordering of Spanish Clitics*. Unpublished Master's Thesis (Texas, 1969).

Walker, Marlene K. "Morpheme Alternants in Spanish Verb Forms," *Language Learning*, 9:3-4 (1959), 33-44.

Wallis, Ethel and William E. Bull. "Spanish Adjective Position: Phonetic Stress and Emphasis," *Hispania*, 33 (August, 1950), 221-229.

Woehr, Richard, "*Acaso, quizá(s), tal vez*: Free Variants?," *Hispania*, 55 (May, 1972), 320-327.

Wolfe, David L. *A Generative-Transformational Analysis of Spanish Verb Forms*. Unpublished Dissertation (Michigan, 1966).

Wonder, John P. "Complementos de adjetivo del genitivo," *Hispania*, 54 (March, 1971), 114-120.

Zamora, Vicente A. *Dialectología española.* Madrid: Editorial Gredos, 1960.

Zdenek, Joseph W. "Another Look at the Progressive," *Hispania*, 55 (September, 1972), 498-499.

Zlotchew, Clark M. "More Thoughts on *lo* and *le*," *Hispania*, 52 (December, 1969), 870-871.

INDEX TO BOOKS AND ARTICLES REVIEWED

This Index is arranged alphabetically by author under the topic headings of the text, and contains the following information: author, title of book/article, and date of publication. The reader should refer to the text entry for complete bibliographic information.

I. GENERAL STUDIES

Barrutia, R., "Linguistics and the Teacher of Spanish and Portuguese" (1969).
———. "Some Misconceptions about the Fundamental Skills Method" (1966).
Bartley, D. and R. L. Politzer, *Practice-Centered Teacher Training: Spanish* (1970).
Brown, M. J., "A FLES Research and Experimental Project" (1965).
Bull, W. E., *Spanish for Teachers: Applied Linguistics* (1965).
———. "We Need a Communications Grammar" (1968).
Cárdenas, D., *Applied Linguistics: Spanish* (1961).
Feldman, D. M. and W. D. Kline, *Spanish: Contemporary Methodology* (1969).
Lado, R., *Linguistics across Cultures: Applied Linguistics for Language Teachers* (1957).
Molina, H., "The Learner, the Teacher, the Grammar and the Method in Designing an Instructional Program" (1971).
Politzer, R. L. and C. N. Staubach, *Teaching Spanish: A Linguistic Orientation* (1961).
Saporta, S., "Applied Linguistics and Generative Grammar" (1966).
Wolfe, D. L., "Some Theoretical Aspects of Language Learning and Language Teaching" (1967).

180

Critical Bibliography

II. TEACHING PHONOLOGY

Barrutia, R., "From Phoneme to Grapheme Audio-lingually" (1964).

———. "Visual Phonetics" (1970).

Beberfall, L., "*Y* and *LL* in Relaxed Spanish Speech" (1961).

Beym, R., "Practical Phonological Orientation for Effective Spoken Spanish" (1960).

Boggs, R. S., *Spanish Pronunciation Exercises* (1954).

Bowen, J. D. and R. P. Stockwell, *Patterns of Spanish Pronunciation: A Drillbook* (1960).

Bowen, J. D., "Teaching Spanish Diphthongs" (1963).

Cárdenas, D., *Introducción a una comparación fonológica del español y del inglés* (1960).

Contreras, H., "Vowel Fusion in Spanish" (1969).

Dalbor, J. B., *Spanish Pronunciation: Theory and Practice* (1969).

Dreher, B. and J. Larkins, "Non-semantic Auditory Discrimination: Foundation for Second Language Learning" (1972).

Estarellas, J., "Problems in Teaching Spanish Pronunciation and Writing by the Audio-lingual Method: A Case Study" (1972).

———, and T. F. Regan, Jr., "Effects of Teaching Sounds as Letters Simultaneously at the Very Beginning of a Basic Foreign Language Course" (1966).

Green, J. R., *Spanish Phonology for Teachers: A Programmed Introduction* (1970).

Hadlich, R. L., J. S. Holton and M. Montes, *A Drillbook of Spanish Pronunciation* (1968).

Hammerly, H., "And Then They Disbelieved Their Ears" (1970).

Matluck, J. L., "The Presentation of Spanish Pronunciation in American Textbooks" (1957).

Mills, D. H., "Why Learn Contrasting Intonation Contours?" (1969).

Navarro Tomás, T., *Manual de pronunciación española* (1957).

Sacks, N. P., "A Study in Spanish Pronunciation Errors" (1962).

———. "Peninsular and American Spanish" (1969).

Stockwell, R. P. and J. D. Bowen, *The Sounds of English and Spanish* (1965).

Wright, L. O., "Five Spanish *R*'s: How to Approach Them" (1962).

III. TEACHING GRAMMAR

Beberfall, L., "Spanish Verb Forms by Conversion" (1963).

Bolinger, D. L., "Reference and Inference: Inceptiveness in the Spanish Preterite" (1963).

———. "Three Analogies" (1961).

Bowen, J. D. and T. Moore, "The Reflexive in English and Spanish: A Transformational Approach" (1968).

Bull, W. E. and E. E. Lamadrid, "Our Grammar Rules Are Hurting Us" (1971).

Carfora, J., "*Lo* and *Le* in American Spanish" (1968).

Cressey, W. W., "Teaching Irregular Present Tense Verb Forms: A Transformational Approach" (1972).

———. "Teaching the Position of Spanish Adjectives: A Transformational Approach" (1969).

Dalbor, J. B., "A Simplified Tagmemic Approach for Teaching Spanish Syntax" (1972).

———. "Temporal Distinctions in the Spanish Subjunctive" (1969).

Dinnes, I. S., "Must All Unclassified Spanish Words Be Memorized for Gender?" (1971).

Douglass, R. T., "Gerundive and Non-Gerundive Forms" (1967).

Farley, R. A. "Sequence of Tenses: A Useful Principle?" (1965).

———. "Time and the Subjunctive in Contemporary Spanish" (1970).

Feldman, D. M., "A Syntactic Verb-Unit in Spanish" (1962).

Fish, G. T., "Adjectives Fore and Aft: Position and Function in Spanish" (1961).

———. "*Lo puede hacer* vs. *puede hacerlo*" (1961).

———. "*Se*" (1966).

———. "Syntactic Equations" (1962).

———. "Two Notes on *Estar*" (1964).

Holton, J. S., "Placement of Object Pronouns" (1960).

Jackson, R. and D. Bolinger, "*Trabajar para*" (1965).

Kiddle, L. B., "A Suggestion for Teaching the Spanish *Tuteo*" (1956-57).

Lozano, A. G., "Non-Reflexivity of the Indefinite *Se* in Spanish" (1970).

Moen, M. E., "The Fable of the Malapropish Affixes" (1966).

Molina, H., "Transformational Grammar in Teaching Spanish" (1968).

Moody, R., "More on Teaching Spanish Adjective Position: Some Theoretical and Practical Considerations" (1971).

Newman, S. W., "Audio-lingualism and the Reversibles" (1963).

Richman, S., "The Translation to Spanish of English Nouns in Juxtaposition" (1969).

Saporta, S., "Problems in the Comparison of the Morphemic Systems of English and Spanish" (1956).

Schmitz, J. R., "The *Se Me* Construction: Reflexive for Unplanned Occurrences" (1966).

Schneer, R. J., "The Future and Conditional of Probability—A Teaching Technique" (1960).

Seelye, H. N., "The Spanish Passive: A Study in the Relation Between Linguistic Form and World-View" (1966).

Stockwell, R. P., J. D. Bowen and J. W. Martin, *The Grammatical Structures of English and Spanish* (1965).

Wilson, R. E., "Polite Ways to Give Orders" (1965).

IV. LISTENING AND SPEAKING

Antoine, G., " 'Conversational Spanish'—A One Year High School Course" (1972).

Kalivoda, T. B., "An Individual Study Course for Facilitating Advanced Oral Skills" (1972).

Nacci, C. N., "Enriching the Audio-lingual Activity in the Classroom" (1965).

Ryan, J., "Spanish Composition and Conversation" (1961).

Segreda, W. and A. Valdman, "Teaching Spoken Spanish in High School and College" (1961).

V. READING AND WRITING

Beberfall, L., "A Note on the *Nuevas Normas de Prosodia y Ortografía* (1959)" (1962).

Blayne, T. C., "Results of Developmental Reading Procedures in First-Year Spanish" (1946).

Bowen, J. D. and R. P. Stockwell, "Orthography and Respelling in Teaching Spanish" (1957).

Calvert, L., "The Role of Written Exercises in an Audio-lingual Program" (1965).

Carsello, C. J. and L. V. Braun, "Rapid Reading Spanish Material" (1972).

Nacci, C. N., "Realizing the Reading Comprehension and Literature Aims via an Audio-lingual Orientation" (1966).

Olstad, C., "Composition in Imitation" (1964).

Sacks, N. P., "The Pattern Drill and the Rationale of the Prosodic and Orthographic Accents in Spanish" (1963).

Savaiano, E., "Does Teaching by the Audio-Lingual Approach Prepare the Student for Reading and Writing?" (1960).

Seelye, H. N. and J. L. Day, "Penetrating the Mass Media: A Unit to Develop Skill in Reading Spanish Newspaper Headlines" (1971).

Teschner, R. V., "The Written Accent in Spanish: A Programmed Lesson" (1971).

VI. DRILLS AND DRILLING

Foster, D. W., "A Model for Drilling Some Points of Grammar" (1965).

Frey, H. J., "Audio-lingual Teaching and the Pattern Drill" (1968).

Gaarder, A. B., "Beyond Grammar and Beyond Drills" (1967).

Golinkin, B. D., "Some Pedagogic Tools for Third-Year College Spanish Classes" (1971).

Hadlich, R. L., "Lexical Contrastive Analysis" (1965).

O'Connor, P., "A Film Strip for Pattern Drill" (1953-54).

VII. METHODOLOGY AND METHOD EVALUATION

Blickenstaff, C. B. and F. J. Woerdehoff, "A Comparison of the Monostructural and Dialogue Approaches to the Teaching of College Spanish" (1967).

Chastain, K. D. and F. J. Woerdehoff, "A Methodological Study Comparing the Audio-Lingual Habit Theory and the Cognitive Code-Learning Theory" (1968).

Guerra, M. H., "Is Conversation Enough? A Reappraisal of Beginning Foreign Language Instruction" (1960).

Maynes, J. O, Jr., "An Experiment to Gauge the Effectiveness of the Audio-lingual Method and the Language Lab" (1962).

Richards, S. E. and J. E. Appel, "The Effects of Written Words in Beginning Spanish" (1956).

Sacks, N. P., "*Modern Spanish* in an Intensive Program for Graduate Students: An Experiment and Some Reflections" (1967)

VIII. MATERIAL EVALUATION

Chastain, K., "Selecting a Basic Text: A Subjective Evaluation" (1971).

Moye del Barrio, M., "Emergence of a Spanish Television Course for FLES" (1965).

Sacks, N. P., "The Art of the Spanish Textbook, 1917-1967" (1967).

Sheppard, D. C., "What Text Shall I Use?" (1960).

Siciliano, E. A., "Common Sense in Our Texts" (1964).

IX. THE LANGUAGE LABORATORY

Barrutia, R., "The Language Laboratory" (1969).

Garnett, N. A., "Making the Language Laboratory Effective" (1967).

Phillips, R., "Using the Tape Recorder to Correct Student Compositions" (1968).

X. PROGRAMED INSTRUCTION

Barrutia, R., "Computerized Foreign Language Instruction" (1970).

———. "A Suggested Automated Branch Program for Foreign Languages" (1964).

Estarellas, J., "The Self-Instructional Foreign Language Program at Florida Atlantic University" (1970).

Turner, R. C., "CARLOS: Computer-Assisted Instruction in Spanish" (1970).

XI. TESTING

Andrade, M., J. L. Hayman, Jr., and J. T. Johnson, Jr., "Measurement of Listening Comprehension in Elementary-School Spanish Instruction" (1963).

Hoge, H. W., "Testing in the Language Laboratory: A Laboratory Experiment in Spanish Pronunciation" (1959).

Holton, J. S., "The Proficiency Ladder" (1963).

Wilkins, G. W., Jr., and and E. L. Hoffman, "The Use of Cognates in Testing Pronunciation" (1964).

Woodford, P. E., "Testing Procedures" (1969).

XII. MISCELLANEOUS

Bull, W. E., "Spanish Word Counts: Theory and Practice" (1950).

Green, J. R., *A Gesture Inventory for the Teaching of Spanish* (1968).

Knowlton, J. F., "The Untranslatable: Translation as a Critical Tool" (1967).